Praise for *Se*

If my house caught fire...
"The *See the Beauty* program has changed the way I look at my own life and has helped me recognize the beauty that has passed me by for years. If my house caught fire and I only had time to save a few things, my *See the Beauty* journal would be at the top of the list."

Author Meg Muldoon

A positive force in a negative world
"My spouse died in early 2017. I can honestly say that Jools Sinclair's *See the Beauty* class helped me through one of the darkest times in my life by reminding me that there is beauty everywhere if we just open our eyes, hearts, and minds to it... I cannot adequately express the importance of this book in our world. Being reminded of the positive in an often negative environment is crucial! Thank you Jools Sinclair for reminding us to see the beauty. I HIGHLY recommend this book."

Debbie Butler

Life changing! *See the Beauty* is a MUST!
"I embarked on this challenge knowing that I suck at art, but I found out I didn't care. There are so many things in life that are beautiful, but we let the negatives take away the focus. I took so much away from this that I constantly seek to find the beauty in each day, whether or not I record it... It is comforting to know that the beauty is there and all we have to do is open our minds to it."

Anna Holmes

A masterpiece
"This book is amazing. I can honestly say this class and book will change the way you see yourself. It helped me redirect my way of thinking. I hope more people will See the Beauty in their own lives. Thank you from the bottom of my heart, Jools."

Sara West

A true gift

As a double cancer survivor myself, I live in gratitude and I see the world in a different way than many people. I was amazed and delighted to see that this book enhances and deepens my own appreciation—and in fact, supplements it wonderfully. Anyone would benefit from reading this book and working through the program. I believe this is especially true for those of us who are illness survivors or trauma survivors; another way to practice thankfulness in life is a wonderful gift.

Marie Maher

Amazing journey through an AMAZING book

... Such a complex world we live in, yet here with this book, Jools simplifies things to a proven basic tenet of life: You live what you believe. If all you see is the big, ugly negative, so will your life be. If you see, smell, touch, taste and hear the beauty that surrounds us all, your life will be filled with beauty. This is a simple concept that Jools guides you to, masterfully. Everyone should get this book and follow the 30-day process... And when it's over, do it again. Buy this book for yourself, your boss, family members or friends. It's a beautiful thing!

Susan Phillips

The BEST self-help book out there

This is the best self help book out there. Take and make time for yourself. So often we don't. Do the assignments and open yourself up to seeing the beauty in your life. If you get behind, which happens, get right back at it as soon as you can. I guarantee you will feel and see a magical change in your life. Well done Jools Sinclair and thank you!

Janice Williams

SEE THE BEAUTY

A 30-Day Celebration of Your Magnificent Life

Jools Sinclair

You Come Too Publishing

See the Beauty: A 30-Day Celebration of Your Magnificent Life
Published by You Come Too Publishing, Tucson, Arizona.

Text Copyright © 2018 by Jools Sinclair.

Printed in the United States of America
First Edition, 2018

ISBN-13: 978-1984223623
ISBN-10: 1984223623 ·

For Joe,
aka Mr. Jools,

For the beauty that you are
and the beauty that we share

Important Note:

Please visit *SeetheBeautyProject.com/art* to look at examples of some of the art, techniques, and projects discussed in this book.

CONTENTS

See the Beauty

A 30-Day Celebration
of Your Magnificent Life

INTRODUCTION

LET'S BEGIN

In beauty I walk
With beauty before me I walk
With beauty behind me I walk
With beauty above me I walk
With beauty around me I walk
It has become beauty again

Navajo Prayer

This 30-day program is a path back to seeing life, your life, as it truly is: amazing, big, and beautiful. It's a practice of "interactive gratitude" that will help you notice and then record the beauty in your life every day, letting you unplug from a negative world and reawaken into a positive one full of grace and appreciation.

Your life is full of beauty right now, even with the credit card debt, the extra 20 pounds, the divorce, the troubling news in the world, the terrible boss, and the car that makes a funny noise when you accelerate. Even in the midst of all the chaos, you are surrounded in beauty. But if you're like most people, you barely know it's there because you've fallen into a habit of focusing on the bad instead of the good.

I know this because that's exactly what I was doing for most of my life. I was living inside a fog and I didn't even know it. It finally dawned on me one day when I returned from a long walk.

It was during a period when I was writing my bestselling mystery series, *Forty-Four*. Life was good. I was making six figures a year for the first time ever, I had fans waiting for my new releases, and I was doing what I had dreamt about since I was a kid—writing for a living. But for some reason I wasn't particularly happy. Despite the money and success, most of the time I was still swept up and focused on the nitty-gritty problems of day-to-day living.

One afternoon after hours of being locked up with my main character, I was eager to escape and get some fresh air. Walks have always been an important part of writing for me, a chance to release endorphins while thinking about plots and scenes. So I slipped on my shoes and headed outside.

After a block or so, I stopped thinking about the story and turned my attention to my sore heels, which had been hurting and didn't seem to be getting any better. This thought led me to thinking about how I probably should go see a doctor, and this thought led to how I had gained weight and didn't want to get on that scale. As I rounded a corner, my brain hopscotched back to the book I was writing, but suddenly veered over to my frustration about how *Forty-Four* had been close to being made into a television series, but had lost out to a zombie show. (No, not *that* zombie show.)

My mind was on a wild ride, Mr. Toad at the wheel with no brakes and plenty of gas. When I turned around and headed back home, it kept going. I thought about obnoxious politicians, annoying celebrities, and about how the housing market had recovered everywhere in the country except the place where I actually owned a house.

When I returned home I drank some water and went over to an open window.

And that's when it hit me.

The blue skies. Warm air. The smell of hot pine needles in the soft wind. It was the end of summer and the bright leaves had just a hint of orange at the edges. Purple wildflowers grew in the yard, red berries cascaded off vines, butterflies fluttered near the grass.

It was a fantastic time in Bend, Oregon, and I had battled snow and ice and cold temperatures for five months to get to this brief oasis of sunshine and warmth. And yet on the walk I had missed all of it, hadn't even given it a second glance.

It was a startling and painful realization. But then I thought of something else.

What if this was happening all the time?

What if I spent most days focused on the negative aspects in life while ignoring the blessings around me?

Not long after, I started a simple daily practice of noticing the beauty in my life and recording it in a journal. And not just natural beauty like sunsets and colorful leaves, but all kinds. Everything that I saw, touched, tasted, heard, smelled, and felt. The beauty of the people I interacted with, the beauty of good writing, the beauty in the books I read and the music I listened to. The beauty in drinking a glass of wine at four o'clock on the deck, the soft fur of my cat at my fingertips.

I wanted to give these moments their proper respect, give them the attention they deserved. I certainly focused a lot on all those bad, grating things, why not spend at least 20 minutes a day thinking about all the good ones?

I made the commitment to sit down in the late afternoon every day with my journal for one month. And because I wanted this new practice to be fun and not just another writing obligation, I bought some nice colored pencils to sketch little illustrations alongside my short entries.

I put all of it in my journal, big moments of beauty and little moments. Everything. The email from a reader who loved my books, red-gold sunsets, cooking *Lasagne alla Bolognese*, the conversation I overheard between two five-year-olds talking about Batman, watching a Dodger game, a full moon rising up over the mountains, impromptu and silly dancing with my husband.

And, as the weeks went by, something magical happened. I started seeing more and more beauty, and it soon felt like I had entered into another world. A world that existed right there beside the negative one. A place that left me feeling happy and appreciative.

And that was how *See the Beauty* was born.

The program is not about slapping a happy face on devastating events or pretending that life is wonderful when you're experiencing difficulties and are in a dark night of the soul. And it's not about picking up a pencil and drawing a flower when everything feels like it's falling apart.

Life is hard. But, if we're honest, most of us would agree that our lives aren't falling apart most of the time. Still, we're in the habit of giving our attention and power over to negativity, a darkness that drains our energy and spirit. This negativity is everywhere, wanting and needing and feeding off the light inside us.

It's on our phones, tablets, and laptops. It's on the television at the gym when we're trying to do a workout and at the hotel breakfast bar. It's in the lunchroom chatter as we refill our coffee mugs. We have a tendency to not only listen to bad news and gossip, but we also spend valuable time reacting to it.

I'm not suggesting that you should remain ignorant or uncaring of the world's woes. What I am saying is that you should be the one in charge of your focus. Not Fox News or CNN. Not the White House. Not Wall Street or Madison Avenue. *You.*

See the Beauty is a simple practice that allows you to step back, unplug, and start giving yourself a little time each day to appreciate your amazing life. And when you do this, you'll begin seeing the following:

- Instead of lack, you'll see the abundance that surrounds you;
- Instead of desire for the things you don't have, you'll feel gratitude for all the wonders that you already possess; and
- Instead of feeling overwhelmed by a mean, crazy, and out-of-control world, you'll begin to see that your own life is really not so mean, so crazy, or so out-of-control but bursting with beauty.

While I can't say that all my problems and habits of negative thinking have vanished since starting this practice years ago, I can tell you that making a conscious effort to notice beauty has helped cultivate a deep reverence and appreciation for my life.

Most days you'll find me sitting at the table in the late afternoon with my journal open and a pencil in hand. It's a routine that I am grateful to have found and am so excited to share with you.

Because the core of the *See the Beauty* program is about love, it is the perfect companion to all religions, philosophies, and beliefs.

So, welcome! I'm so glad that you're here on this journey.

Jools Sinclair

WHAT YOU'LL NEED TO GET STARTED

Okay, so here's what you'll need before you begin the *See the Beauty* 30-day program:

A blank-page "sketch" journal

In this journal you will be recording the beauty that you notice throughout your day. A couple of things to keep in mind when choosing your journal are size and paper quality.

First, size. Don't go too big, unless it really calls to you. I use a 5 x 8.25-inch journal. It's easy to carry around and the small size gives me the confidence that I'll be able to fill the blank page on a daily basis. On days when I see extra beauty, I use an additional page or two. So pick a size that works for you.

You'll also have to think about the thickness of the paper. If you're using colored pencils, then regular paper is fine. But if you want to use colored-pencil watercolors or markers, you'll need to get a journal with thicker paper.

Your choice of art medium

You will be adding illustrations to your journal entries so you'll need to decide what type of art supplies to use. Personally I love colored pencils, but use whatever calls to you. Here are a few other suggestions:

- watercolor pencils;
- markers;

- regular pencils;
- crayons;
- pastels;
- watercolors or other paints;
- gel pens;
- charcoal (if you're willing to put up with a little mess);
- or a combination of some of the above.

Adding both background color and illustrations to your daily entries is an important component of the program, even if you opt to only draw gray skies and red hearts. The act of creating art in your *See the Beauty* journal will help you experience the wonder in your life on a deeper level. I realize that for many, the fear of drawing might be right up there with death and public speaking, but I promise it won't be that bad. Please don't skip the art part. Just know that your journal is a safe place to create and you won't ever have to share your entries with anyone else (unless you want to).

For now, if the idea of art causes queasiness, tell yourself that you really are capable of adding some background color, drawing an abstract flower or two, or resorting to stick figure representations of your spouse and children.

A "tracker" to use during the day

You'll need a way to help remember those moments of beauty that you see daily. It's so easy to say, "Oh, I won't forget this!" and then hours later when you sit down at your journal, you've completely forgotten. Here are a few ideas that can help you keep track of the beauty:

- Use your phone to take photos. Simply take pictures of the beauty you see and scroll through the shots right before you sit down to make an entry in your journal. (Just make sure to turn off your phone during your journal time.)
- Use the audio recorder on your phone and leave yourself messages. I use this often when I'm out on walks and it works great.
- Use a small notebook and write down the beauty you see throughout the day. Old school all the way, but effective and

easy. (I also like to have one on my nightstand so that I can write down some of those beautiful moments that may have happened after my journaling session.)

Time

You'll need at least 20 minutes, preferably at the same time every day. I like the time right before dinner best, after most of my day is done, before sitting down to eat. I know others who like to journal right after dinner when their kids are doing homework. Others bring it along to dance or soccer practices, drawing in the car. And then there are some people who take their journal to bed with them to do their entries. It's just a matter of finding the right time that will work for you.

Make sure that you are in a quiet place with no distractions. Shut your laptop and turn off your phone. Treat this time as sacred, a small part of the day that you're setting aside to appreciate your magnificent life.

Chances are there will be a day now and again when you don't even have 20 minutes to journal. This is what I do at those times. I'll go ahead and open my journal anyway, even if it's just for a minute or two. I'll quickly jot down a few things and catch up the next day or even on the weekend when I have a little more time for the art. It's not something you'll want to do regularly, but occasionally it's great for "saving" the daily habit. A little beauty is infinitely better than none.

A judgment-free state of mind

For a lot of people, picking up a colored pencil or a paintbrush often unleashes a vile inner critic. But when you sit down with your journal, tell Negative Nancy to wait outside because you are in a judgment-free zone.

Creating art in this program is about fun and relaxation, not stress. You don't have to be, nor are you expected to be, an "artist." All you need is a willingness to shut off the critical voices so that you are free to create in peace.

Your *See the Beauty* journal deserves to be treated with reverence. And to be able to do that successfully you'll need to leave the critic on the other side of the door.

That's it. You're ready to *See the Beauty!*

JOURNALING STYLES

Everybody is different, so it makes sense that everybody will have their own style when it comes to writing and drawing in their *See the Beauty* journal. There is no right way to make the entries, other than showing up daily and doing the work.

Over the years I've tried the different ways listed below but have always gravitated back to my original style. On one page I'll jot down a few different "points of beauty" and draw small illustrations next to each one. On the adjoining or opposite page, I'll list any additional beauty in my day, including quotes I may have read or heard, books that I'm enjoying, music that has moved me, and even the friendly conversation with the woman who delivers my mail.

Below are a few approaches to get you started. Try some over the course of the first week and then settle into the one that you like best.

- *Four or five beautiful moments with small illustrations.* For example, I might write "walked three miles in Saguaro National Park early," with a picture of some of those majestic saguaro cacti along with the sun rising. Then, I'll have a short phrase about meeting my daughter for lunch, and I might draw a small picture of two smiling faces and a pizza. You get the idea.

- *Fewer beautiful moments with larger illustrations.*
- *One moment with one illustration.* I really like this concept, but have never been able to stick with it consistently. Author Meg Muldoon, on the other hand, loves to use watercolor pencils to capture the one special moment of beauty that rocked her day. Meg is an artist and enjoys combining the practice of seeing the beauty with her art making. There are just a few words accompanying her entries, sometimes only a title. The final result, a calendar-style collection of her month, is quite spectacular. There are a few things to keep in mind, however, if you're interested in this style. First, it puts a lot of pressure on the art. If you find yourself having a few creatively-challenged days, it might easily discourage you from the entire practice. Also, this technique is more time consuming.
- *Heavy on words, light on art.* Some people are writers by nature. If that's you, feel free to write as much as you want, but just make sure to add a little color or a few doodles here and there.

As you begin making entries and the days go by, you will discover what you like best and develop your own personal style in your *See the Beauty* journal.

A note about taking photos:
Sometimes students will say, "I'm really good at snapping pictures with my phone. Can't I arrange my cool photos in an online journal and just call it good? I mean, photography is art, right?"

While taking, developing, and editing photographs is definitely art and can be an awesome activity (any time spent capturing moments of beauty in your life is its own reward), this program is most effective when you create the art by hand.

WHY ART?

Sometimes I get questions from people who really want to sign up and take a *See the Beauty* class, but have issues with the art component. Their comments and questions go something like this:

> *"Why art, Jools?"*
> *"Do I really have to draw?"*
> *"I hate art! It reminds me of my ceramics teacher in seventh grade when she gave me a C- on my penguin."*
> *"Art is embarrassing!"*
> *"I love journaling. I'll just write extra pages every day instead."*
> *"Uh, last I checked, we live in the 21st century where smartphones rule the world. I'll just take some pictures, m'kay?"*

You don't have to do art. You don't have to do anything you don't want to do.

But...

You really should.

See the Beauty includes art for a reason. As it turns out, producing art is really quite good for us.

It's been scientifically proven that engaging in the art process reduces anxiety, makes new connections between brain cells (and that helps with something called brain plasticity), enhances problem-solving skills, improves creative thinking, reduces sadness, stimulates the brain to grow more neurons, reduces stress, helps people forget their problems for a while, and encourages both hemispheres of the brain to communicate with each other.

But the most important part of all this is that to get these benefits, you only have to participate in the process. The end result doesn't matter one bit. Once you pick up the paintbrush, push the pencil across the page, or dig your hands in the clay, you've won.

All you have to do is learn to put aside the self-judgment and criticism for a few minutes each day while you draw like no one's watching. (Because they're not.)

TIPS FOR SUCCESS

See the Beauty will help you celebrate your life. And because people usually need at least 30 days to establish a habit, the program is divided into daily segments, each with a short essay, an assignment, and an extra credit exercise.

Ideally, you should do the reading and the 20-minute assignment every day. The essays are all short and illustrate a point, something that I've learned on my own path to seeing the beauty. There is always the same "required" assignment for each day, and that is to simply focus on the beauty of *your* day and do an entry in the journal. The extra credit is there for you if you have the time or inclination.

One approach is to read the essay in the morning and do your entry at night. Another option is to do the reading right before working on the journal. Of course, you could jump ahead and read more than one essay at a time. Just make sure to come back for the daily assignments.

Your journal entries are the most important part of *See the Beauty*. Stopping to reflect on the many blessings in your life and taking the time to fill your soul with gratitude and appreciation is what it's all about. If you never read the essays or do the extra credit, but just open your journal for 30 straight days and record the beauty in your world, you will have succeeded.

The extra credit exercises at the end of each day are completely optional. They are there should you want to go a little deeper. They are not there to shame you if you don't have the time or the desire to do them. Do the exercises that call to you. Or don't. Hopefully, these 30 days will merely serve as an introduction to a lifelong journey of seeing the beauty. Perhaps, this time around you might do a few extra credit assignments or none at all. That's fine. When you return to the program in the future you might be ready for more.

Here are a few tips for success...

- Do your journaling at the same time each day.
- Have all your supplies ready before you begin.
- Don't stress over word choice or artistic quality. Approach each entry with a relaxed, carefree attitude—not another chore or something to check off a to-do list.
- If you miss an entry, get right back to it the very next day.

A word about sharing... Don't. At least not at first.

See the Beauty is a very personal journey, and it's your journey. So be cautious about sharing your journal. It's natural and part of our DNA to want attention and recognition, but people can be cruel—sometimes without meaning to be. And that can work both ways. You might not want to hear that the petals on your rose look like daggers or that your dog looks like an armadillo. And the person you share with might get their feelings hurt if you don't draw them to their liking, or leave them out altogether. Hurt feelings will discourage you and extinguish the practice quicker than dropping a match into the ocean.

So either learn to have fun with it all (i.e., not have an ego invested in their opinion) or don't share.

SETTING YOUR MORNING INTENTION

Starting a new habit like *See the Beauty* is about change. Changing the way you do things, instilling a new pattern among very old ones. And while this is easy to do for the first few days when you're pumped up, it can be harder to sustain as time goes on.

That's why it's important to set an intention every morning.

But before I go any further, I need to tell you about canoe trips.

There was a time when my family and I took long canoe camping trips, staying out in the wilderness for weeks at a time. The process would begin months earlier. We would choose where to go, make reservations, compile long supply lists, gather everything, and pack up before finally heading out. Sometimes we hired an outfitter to drive us to a remote place in the middle of nowhere and leave us on a desolate shoreline. And for the next few weeks, we'd paddle on rivers and lakes, navigate down wild rapids, drift through thick forests, float under blazing suns, and portage all our gear through overgrown paths between bodies of water. We braved storms, saw bears up close and personal, listened to loons at dusk, and watched northern lights dance on crisp, cold skies before falling asleep.

Every morning during these epic adventures, we'd take out our maps and look ahead at where we were going that day, even though we already basically knew the route. By doing this daily activity, pointing our canoes in the right direction, we could be *fairly* certain that we'd arrive not only at the right campsite each night, but also at the take-out point by the end of our trip.

Setting the intention for the day by studying the map was a key to our success. And the same is true for you now as you begin this journey.

By setting an intention each morning when you wake up, you'll greatly increase your chances of arriving at your destination, of seeing the daily beauty in your life.

It's a simple act and yet extremely powerful. It will help remind you to notice the taste of good coffee, the trees swaying in the breeze, your dog's happiness when you walk through the door. So before you begin this program, come up with a morning intention phrase or mantra that you can use for the next 30 days.

This is mine: "Today I'm going to look for all the beauty that surrounds me."

It's short, easy to remember, and helps remind me of what I'm planning to do that day. I'm setting my focus.

You can use this phrase or come up with your own. The important thing is to say it every morning during the next 30 days to help you get into the habit of looking for beauty everywhere you go.

Other things to consider...

• If you want to use a longer intention quote, keep a copy of it on your nightstand or taped to your bathroom mirror so it's easy to read out loud when you first wake up.
• Soft, gentle background music can be added for extra inspiration.
• You can be anywhere, like a garden or rooftop or a corner of your house that you've set up with some favorite items. I know people who have created shrines for this purpose using small water features, Buddhas, or Mary statues.

My advice would be to keep it simple. Establish a morning intention routine that will be easy to follow, something that will point your day in the right direction.

Toward beauty.

CAN WE AGREE?

See the Beauty is for everyone.

That being said, while not everyone will or should agree as to what beauty is (more on this later), there is a basic premise at the heart of this program that cannot be ignored.

Beauty is love.

There is no beauty in hurting yourself or others. Beauty cannot be found in small-mindedness, pettiness, or hatred. There is no beauty in racism or misogyny or intolerance or oppression.

So, while everyone has their own interpretation of beauty, this program isn't a justification for seeing beauty in evil.

Seeing the beauty is about love.

Enough said.

See the Beauty

A 30-Day Celebration
of Your Magnificent Life

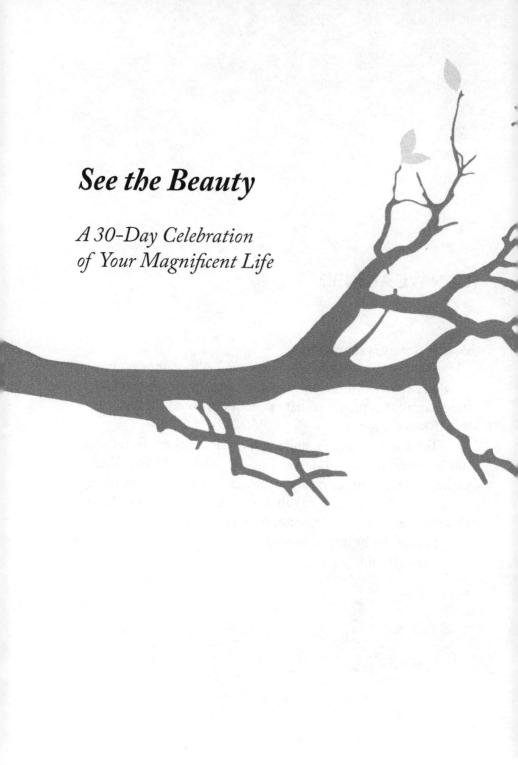

THE 30-DAY PROGRAM

DAY 1: OPEN YOUR EYES, OPEN YOUR HEART

Look around. Look at what we have. Beauty is everywhere—you only have to look to see it.

Bob Ross

Your life is surrounded by beauty, but if you're like most people you haven't gotten into a regular habit of noticing it. And that's what this class is about. Spending a little time each day focusing on the amazing moments in your life.

Every day for 30 days, you will record some of the beauty you encounter in your sketch journal. And while this might seem like a simple activity, I guarantee that doing it will create profound appreciation and change in your life.

The beauty I am talking about here is with you right now. It's not in the future when you've found the perfect spouse or job or moisturizer. It's not when you write the novel that soars on the *New York Times* bestseller list, or when you're able to buy a house on a hill, or when you finally are a size 6, or when you can go on that dream vacation to the Caribbean and sit on a white sandy beach pounding back Bahama Mamas.

Your life is full of beauty now. Beauty that you can see, hear, taste, touch, and feel. It's everywhere—in nature, people, events, books, music, sports, food. So, as you go through your day, notice all the wonder that you come across.

It's all right there, waiting for you.

Today's Assignment:

1. Set your morning intention shortly after waking up. If you've forgotten, do it whenever you remember.
2. Later in the afternoon or evening, in your journal record some of those beautiful moments you've had in your day. Add an illustration or two, but if you're not comfortable drawing right now just go ahead and use your colored pencils for backgrounds, swirls, stick figures, or smiley faces.

Extra Credit: Write a Letter to Yourself

Write a letter to yourself, answering the following questions:

- How much appreciation do you feel on a daily basis?
- Why are you doing this program?
- What are some negative beliefs you have regarding your life right now?
- What are you hoping to achieve by the end of these 30 days?

Write this letter on a separate piece of paper that can be tucked away in the back pocket of your journal (or taped if there is no pocket). On Day 30 you'll return to the letter and read it.

DAY 2: DRAW LIKE A FOURTH GRADER

Every child is an artist. The problem is how to remain an artist once we grow up.

Pablo Picasso

I loved teaching fourth grade. The students were eager and excited. They were old enough to have their own insights and opinions, but young enough to consider the other side. They were thrilled with science experiments, books, social studies, and recess. They supported each other. And on the whole, they were great listeners and doers, and that made for a great teaching environment.

Whenever possible I incorporated art into assignments because most children love art. Painting, drawing, sculpting. Watercolors, clay, colored pencils. I noticed early on that if I could bring art into the curriculum the students were naturally more engaged, so I made sure that they had a lot of opportunities to create. Not only did they read books, they made posters of the characters and put them up around the school. Not only did they research and write about a favorite animal, they drew polar bears and leopards onto the borders of their reports. They made Native American villages out of twigs, leaves, clay, and paint, illustrating the diversity of housing structures not just the cliché tepees. They built Oregon Trail wagons out of wood and cloth.

Art brought their learning and understanding to a deeper level, and they usually had a lot of fun. For them the creative process was natural and a huge part of who they were. They loved creating and sharing and seeing their classmates' projects. When it came to art, the students had wide open hearts and minds.

That is, until fifth grade.

One year I looped up to the next grade with the same class and since it was my very first time teaching fifth graders, I didn't see it coming.

The change.

In fifth grade the very same students suddenly became shy and self-conscious about their creations and didn't like sharing anymore. As the year progressed, many didn't even want to do art because they knew that the others would be watching and judging. And they *were* watching and judging, quietly sizing up the projects and comparing them to their own.

In fifth grade as a group they decided what a tree—and pretty much everything else—"should" look like. Art was defined now, and the class decided that most of them had no skill and just shouldn't do it.

In fifth grade the students took that path into the dark forest of judgment and started to listen to those negative voices that told them they "sucked" at art. That forest is where they began to lose their confidence, caring more about what others thought. And in doing so, many put down the colored pencils and paint brushes forever.

It was sad to see. I hoped that one day they would be able to find their way back and once again draw like a fourth grader.

So for today, let your inner artist run free. Add color and line and shape to the pages in your *See the Beauty* journal. Draw cats and dogs and horses, moons and mountains. The enchiladas you made for dinner. Stick people. Your son playing hockey in the backyard.

Remember that art is expression, your expression, and this art is about you losing yourself while you appreciate those beautiful moments in your day. Play!

Today's Assignment:

1. Set your intention early this morning.
2. Draw like a fourth grader as you record beauty in your journal.

Extra Credit: New Job Exercise

This exercise will expand the way you think about color. Pretend that you've just been hired at the Sherman Gilliams Paint Company. Your job is to come up with whimsical new names for the colors below. For example, instead of just red, it's *Roses at Twilight Red*, instead of plain green, it's *Van Gogh Green*. Be creative and have fun! Name paint colors however you wish, after favorite times of the day, favorite characters from a book, a scene out of a movie (*Casablanca Mauve, Elizabeth Bennet Blue, Out of the Past Gray*). Record the new names you've created along with swatches of color in your journal.

Here is the list of colors you've been assigned: red, yellow, green, blue, purple, pink, brown, black, white, and orange. Feel free to add more if you find yourself inspired.

DAY 3: WHERE TO FIND IT

Be happy in the moment, that's enough. Each moment is all we need, not more.

Mother Teresa

Where will you look for beauty today? Here are a few questions that will help bring the wonder of your life into better focus:

- What kind of beauty is in the people that are around you today? (A colleague who brought you tea this morning, the excitement in your daughter's face when she told you about her soccer practice, an email from a lost friend, your neighbor bringing up your trash bin, the guy who showed you road kindness instead of rage.)
- What kind of beauty is in the nature that surrounds you? (A sunrise, birds, mountains, trees, the purple and blue sky at twilight, a glowing orange moon, spring snowflakes twirling in the air, a fierce wind blowing through a field of long grass, rain, leaves chasing you down the street on a crisp autumn day.)
- What kind of beauty do you hear? (A favorite song that comes on the radio, a voice on the phone that causes your heart to flutter, the sound of your car engine turning over when you were sure that the battery was dead.)

Beauty is everywhere if you know where to look.

Today's Assignment:

1. Set your morning intention.
2. Find the beauty of your day and record it in your journal later.

Extra Credit: Make a List of 10 Things You Love Doing

In your journal make a list of 10 things you love doing. Be specific. For example, if you enjoy going on long bike rides, write about where you love to go. If you like staying up late watching movies, note what kinds of movies you watch. If pub crawls are your thing, write about your favorite ales (if you can remember). Add some color and/or illustrations.

Take this exercise a step further by scheduling one of these activities for some time this next month.

DAY 4: CUTE BABIES AND SAWDUST

Beauty is in the eye of the beholder.

Proverb

I was standing at the checkout line at TJ Maxx with my oldest daughter last November, my arms filled with green and red wrapping paper, Italian chocolates, soft socks, and a white sweater with glittery snowflakes embroidered on the sleeves. As we waited, I noticed a young mother up ahead with her baby.

"Oh, my God," I whispered to Cassandra. "Look at that super cute baby!"

This baby was beautiful. She had dark tufts of soft hair and smiled at everything and everybody with pink heart-shaped lips. She was full of fun and light and happiness.

"Isn't she just the cutest?" I said again.

Cassandra finally glanced up from her phone, found the baby in question, and shrugged.

"Sure," she said. "I guess."

She wasn't being mean, just honest. Babies have never spoken to her in the same way that they speak to me. Cassandra doesn't find them particularly beautiful like I do. Her thing is funny animal videos and taking photos of her dogs to post online.

But it made me smile nonetheless, as it reminded me that everyone has their own definition of beauty.

My daughter finds beauty in so many other things that wouldn't make it into my journal, like power tools and sawdust and piles of free wood by the side of the road. She finds beauty in spending hours in her shop, creating and building magnificent art.

Even though we have common threads as human beings, we're all so different. We each walk the world in our own shoes, having our own unique experiences that give us our own unique perspectives on life. We each look different, have different thoughts, have different hopes and dreams, have different interpretations.

And when it comes to beauty, we each have our very own definition of what makes the cut.

A giant jackrabbit sitting underneath a saguaro cactus is beautiful to me, as is the sound of a paddle pushing through lake water on a warm summer day. For me, watching millions of people marching all over the world for women's equality is incredibly moving. The smell of chiles roasting on the streets of Santa Fe, looking for agates on a deserted beach, and watching clouds fat with snow rolling in are all so beautiful to me that I sometimes feel like Joe Cocker.

There is so much beauty in your amazing life. The more you let it in, the bigger your life will be.

Today's Assignment:

1. Set your morning intention.
2. Spend at least 20 minutes with your journal capturing those moments of beauty that you've noticed throughout your day.

Extra Credit: Heart of the Matter

Supplies needed: a large sheet of blank paper, colored pencils, pens, or crayons.

This exercise is a nice way of getting a visual portrait of who you are and what's important to you. You'll be making a heart that will represent you and all the things that you love.

- First, make a list of the things that matter most to you, the things closest to your heart. (For example, family and friends, cooking risotto, Italian opera, skiing, kayaking, writing novels, walking and hiking, snow, sunshine, birds, pine trees, colorful autumn leaves, snorkeling, chocolate chip cookies, road trips.)
- Next, draw a large heart on a large piece of paper.
- Transfer the items from your list onto different parts of the heart, leaving room for small illustrations.
- Add background color(s).

This activity takes a while, so don't feel compelled to finish it in one sitting. But when you're done, take a look at it. Is it a good representation of who you are? Would it tell "your story" if a stranger looked at it?

DAY 5: BEAUTY IS EVERYWHERE

When you realize how perfect everything is you will tilt your head back and laugh at the sky.

The Buddha*

Beauty is everywhere.

It's in the golden leaves shivering at dawn, it's in the big, blue sky, the snow-dusted mountain tops. It's in the soft afternoon light, in the sunbeams filtering through the willows, in the hawk flying overhead, surfing the breeze. It's in the rain, gently kissing your hair or drumming down on the roof of your car as you crank the heater. It's in the way the sidewalk smells after the storm has passed. It's in the fire crackling in the fireplace and the way the shallots give themselves to the butter in the pan.

Beauty is in the book that you stayed up late to read, that insanely sweaty workout that made you feel like an elite athlete, in that old song that moved you to tears.

It's in light displays in windows, it's in dancing candle flames, in the smell of freshly baked bread wafting out the door of a bakery. It's in that first cup of coffee of the day, and in the one after that. It's in the eyes of your lover when his heart is beating next to yours.

Beauty is in your cat's meow and in your dog's wagging tail. Beauty is when you love something so much you're sure that your heart can't survive it.

Beauty is everywhere, in spring blossoms and roadrunners darting through the yard. It's in the way Manu Ginobili plays basketball.

Beauty is in the food that you dream about, the gnocchi in sage butter, the coho salmon on the grill, that green chile burger at your favorite pub. It's in that glass of Chianti on a Thursday afternoon.

Beauty is in doing those things that make you happiest. It's in traveling and cooking, swimming and singing and painting and writing. It's in learning new things, and lacing up an old pair of skates.

Beauty is in the coyote howling across a black night, and it's in autumn owls calling out to each other beneath a full moon. It's in the snake in the tall grass catching the mouse. It's in the mouse getting away to live another day.

It's in the way your husband takes your hand on a cold, dark night and leads you home.

Beauty is in the way things are right now. In memories of a time when they were better. And in the promise that the best is yet to come.

Beauty is in everything that reminds you of the love in your life.

Today's Assignment:

1. Set your morning intention.
2. See the beauty that surrounds you and record it later in your journal.

Extra Credit: Write a "Beauty is..." Poem

Write your own free verse poem about beauty. Use the words, "Beauty is..." to start each line and complete the sentences with specific examples from your own life.

Write at least 10 lines.

Because it's a "free verse" poem, you don't have to worry about rhyming or any other formal pattern. Just let the words flow.

Copy the final version into your journal.

*It's very possible that Buddha never actually said this. Laugh anyway.

DAY 6: A SACRED SPACE

Your sacred space is where you can find yourself again and again.
Joseph Campbell

As you go forward in your *See the Beauty* practice, it's important to remember that your journal is a sacred place. *Your* sacred place. A place to reflect, interpret, and record the beauty in your life. A place to have a little fun with art while you expand those incredible moments into even more moments.

So before you open up your journal and share it with people, keep in mind that there might be that someone who is critical of purple trees or wonders why there are 15 players on your soccer field. Or someone who is a real stickler on spelling and looks horrified as she reads over those creative words that you've used.

Just be aware that sharing comes with a risk.

Today's Assignment:

1. Set your morning intention.
2. See the beauty in your day and record it in your journal.

Extra Credit: *Suiseki*

Go outside today and try some *Suiseki*, the ancient Japanese art of stone appreciation. You're looking for rocks that suggest natural scenes, animals, or figures. It's kind of like that game you played as a kid, lying in the grass, looking for shapes up in the clouds. It's basically the same concept in *Suiseki,* except you'll be looking down at rocks and stones.

For this practice, rocks should never be modified. When you find one (or two), bring it home, draw a picture of it in your journal, and display the rock in a special place.

DAY 7: IT'S IN THE DETAILS

It doesn't matter if things are going the way you want them, stop and pause, and raise your glass to the delicious opportunity life is giving you right now. You'll never get that moment back again.

Rabbi Jack Kalla

I'm not detail oriented, at least not by nature. Most of the time, I'm the type of person who sees the proverbial forest and not so many of the trees. For example, if you were to ask me what I did yesterday, I would probably say, "I worked on my book, took a lunchtime stroll, went shopping, and cooked dinner."

But as the old saying goes, God is in the details. And so is good writing. So when I sit down at the computer to write my novels, I really have to make a point of *seeing* those trees.

Yesterday, I didn't just work on my book, I wrote a 1000-word essay on creativity. I didn't just go shopping, I went to the Eddie Bauer outlet looking for a rain jacket because my old one makes me break out in a sweat. And I didn't just cook, I made an Indian curry dish to which I added extra garlic and cayenne pepper so it would have a kick. Another detail I might mention here is that I consider cooking, when done right, to be very spiritual. And I might even mention that sometimes I get nervous, constantly tasting and adjusting the seasonings before finally turning down the flame, saying a little prayer, and letting the flavors meld.

And as for my stroll, it wasn't just an ordinary walk. I walked over to a small farm where Yanny the Yak lives. I love seeing Yanny, as well as the three alpacas and two goats that share his reddish brown barn and field. If I wanted to add in another detail here, I'd tell you that the goats are really old and like to bleat at me, especially if I show up during their midday feeding.

All of those extra details help to tell a better story.

How does all this relate to seeing the beauty?

The essence of this entire program is about slowing down and paying more attention to the beautiful details of your life. Looking closer at flowers and trees and sunsets. And at the art we humans create. A painting, a song, a fine meal. It's about taking the time to appreciate the coworker who leaves Hershey's Kisses on everyone's desk each Monday, that movie you watched with your kids, the one that had you laughing for the first time all week. That run through the forest that left you breathless.

Details are important. They paint a picture, making the story bigger, more real, something we can almost touch.

Start making an effort to include more details in your entries. When you look back over your journal, it will be all those specific things that will bring a huge smile to your face.

Look closer at your own life and you'll see, really see, how amazing it is.

Today's Assignment:

1. Set your morning intention.
2. For today's entry, remember to add more details, either in words or art or both.

Extra Credit: Georgia O'Keeffe Pastel Drawing

In this extra credit assignment you are going to draw a flower, focusing on the details.

- First, you'll need a large piece of paper (I like to square it off for this activity), a pencil, pastels (if you don't have pastels, use colored pencils or watercolor pencils), and a flower.

• Give yourself plenty of time to study the flower.
• Using a pencil, sketch exactly what you see, drawing the intricate details. Draw it big like Georgia O'Keeffe. (You might want to look up some of her work on the Internet if you're not familiar with her.)
• Have a goal of making your flower touch all four sides of the paper.
• Don't leave the background white. I usually draw a blue sky peeking out from behind my giant flower.

DAY 8: BAD ART HAPPENS

Everybody needs beauty as well as bread...

John Muir

I sat down the other day looking through my own *See the Beauty* journal when I came across a page that I really didn't like.

It was back when I had tried out some new watercolor wax crayons and had added too much water so that the blues bled into the greens, and the red washed away the yellow. I had drawn a bunch of different hearts, but even those had a strange, weird shape to them. In addition the page had gotten so wet that it dried all funky and didn't sit right.

As the days passed, that bad art really started bugging me more and more. Most of my journal was filled with mountain ranges and ristras and stark mesquite trees and javelinas and the faces of the people I love. Looking at the collection it was clear that my art skills had improved over time. That is, until I came across that particular watercolor page.

I decided that the only solution was to rip it out and pretend like it had never happened.

But then I remembered back to when I had done stuff like that before in other journals, and how there was always that ragged edge left behind that I could never completely destroy. And how the edge always reminded me exactly of what had been there before, kind of like a haunting.

So I ended up leaving the bad art alone and moved on.

After a few weeks, much to my surprise, something astounding happened.

Although the page was still kind of ugly, I realized that the lessons it was teaching me were really quite beautiful.

First of all, it reminded me that my art was always a process and not a product. The art I was doing in my journal wasn't heading to a museum or gallery or into a frame for the wall. It wasn't meant to. It was a creative time that allowed me to immerse myself in color for 20 minutes or so as I recorded the beauty of my day, a time to create. It was meant to offer relief after writing all day and to remember to appreciate my life. The end result wasn't supposed to matter, and this particular bad art really helped teach me that.

It also illustrated that growth rarely happens in a linear line, going directly from point A to point B. As you learn something new, there are times when you leap forward and other times when you fall back. It's all natural.

The ugly art also reminded me that it's good to try something new and to take a risk.

Too often I'm a creature of habit. But as Hannibal Lector's mother told him, trying something new is important. (I kid.)

And finally the bad art helps me to remember to be more accepting, more allowing of the things in the world and inside me that are not to my liking. I'm still working on this lesson, but I'm glad it's there in my *See the Beauty* journal so I can ponder away at it some more.

Today's Assignment:

1. Set your morning intention of seeing the beauty in your day.
2. See the beauty and record it later in your journal.

Extra Credit: Dance, Dance, Dance

For today's extra credit choreograph an interpretive dance representing your day. Add music if you think it will help. Good luck!

DAY 9: MORE OF THIS, LESS OF THAT

No one can possess an afternoon of rain beating against the window, or the serenity of a sleeping child, or the magical moment when the waves break on the rocks. No one can possess the beautiful things of this Earth, but we can know them and love them. It is through such moments that God reveals himself to mankind.

Paulo Coelho

I was having lunch with one of my friends the other day when she steered our conversation down a gloomy path and began talking about taxes. For her, it was going to be a terrible tax year because she made a lot of money in her business the year before and now the government wanted its pound of flesh.

Then we both laughed because we knew how lucky she was to be in that situation, at least in a big picture sort of way.

I understood what she was saying though, because I've been in that same exact spot myself. Back when *Forty-Four* went viral, I also had to pay a lot of taxes. But lately, because both my writing and sales have slowed down quite a bit, I don't have the same kinds of tax issues as my friend.

Until that moment, my recent lack of fiscal success had left me feeling troubled and even fearful at times. But as we sat there, drinking wine and laughing about life, I had a shift in my thinking and began to contemplate the bright side of my own situation.

I mean, even with the financial roller coaster I had been on these last few years, I still ate delicious food, lived with my awesome family, had great long talks with my husband, traveled to different places I'd never been before, caught up with old friends through emails, started teaching a class that I really love, did lots of sketching and drawing and art-making, read a lot of great books, saw some really good movies, took long walks, moved to the desert on a new adventure, stopped going to my smelly gym, did lots of swimming, learned about things like palo verde trees and monsoons and that cicadas have the ability to sweat.

And then I thought about how important it had been to take a break from writing, because after finishing my series, I was exhausted and more than a little burned out. And then I thought how kind of amazing it was that I now had all these new projects that I was excited about, including some new book ideas.

And none of this great stuff was taxable!

It was a new way of looking at my situation, but who's to say that it wasn't the way I should have been looking at it all along? Why was it so easy for me to view certain things, like less money coming in, with fear and dread instead of thinking that maybe there was some good underneath it all?

Why not focus more on my blessings and less on what I lacked? Why not stress less and *fun more*? Why not spend more time talking with friends and less time thinking about snakes, taxes, and politicians?

It could very well be the key to life.

More of this, less of that.

Today's Assignment:

1. Set your morning intention.
2. See the beauty of your day and record it later in your journal.

Extra Credit: Day and Night

Set aside time today to visit a place—any place of your choosing as long as it's safe. Visit sometime during the day and then again at night. How does it look in the different light? What differences do you notice? Does the air smell different? Is it crowded or quiet? Does the mood feel different? Which visit did you like better? Why? Write about it in your journal.

DAY 10: BIG MOMENTS AND LITTLE MOMENTS

Love is the bridge between you and everything.

Rumi

Sometimes those big moments of beauty have a million little moments sitting there right beside them.

Take for example the day I met Bruce Springsteen, my favorite don't-stop-till-you-drop, rock and roll idol. With many strokes of luck, mystery, and love, I was one of the few fans holding a ticket to the "Meet and Greet Bruce" event at the Tattered Cover bookstore in downtown Denver one blistering-cold morning.

I was beyond excited. But first, I better backtrack a little and explain how big this moment really was for me.

Back in the day, before smartphones and Stubhub, you had to earn your ticket to a Springsteen concert. You had to earn it by doing a little praying and a whole lot of waiting as you stood in line on a dirty sidewalk before dawn at a Ticketmaster location, your pockets stuffed with cash. But all this was by no means a guarantee of success. All the tickets for the concert were released across the city at once, so you could only hope that the people in front of you and the employees handling the transactions were fast, and that the ones at the other locations were slow. And a few more concerns were in play too, like did I have enough skills to keep a conversation going for hours with my new boyfriend? (I guess I did because we later got married.)

Over the years Bruce has been a big part of my life. I bought his LPs back when vinyl ruled, and then bought his CDs and mp3s. I've been to concerts, watched documentaries and interviews, and even did a "Bruce Tour" in Asbury Park, New Jersey, where I walked along the boardwalk and had my picture taken in front of Madam Marie's. I've danced to his music with both of my daughters when they were babies, and danced with them decades later at a concert, all of us dressed in bright orange T-shirts with "Johnstown Company" logos printed on the front.

So after all the songs, miles, and years, I just knew that the meet-and-greet event was going to be a really big, beautiful moment.

But after a few hours of standing there waiting with a wild and hungry heart, it came to me that I had already experienced so much beauty and I hadn't even met Bruce yet.

Like the beauty of my oldest daughter discovering that he was coming to the bookstore and that the tickets would be going on sale the next day. And the beauty of how that next day she and my husband sat side by side at their laptops, trying to buy them. And the beauty of my husband refusing to give up even when he was booted off the site over and over and over again. And the beauty of how he finally was able to make a purchase, even if it was only for one ticket. And the beauty of how everybody in my family immediately said, "That ticket goes to Mom." And the beauty in how my youngest daughter insisted on paying for it, just because.

There was also the beauty of luck, because although we didn't know it at the time, getting one of the 1000 tickets available was a longshot. There were 20 times that many people trying to meet Bruce, so many in fact that it had caused the website to crash.

There was beauty in catching a ride into the city that morning with my son-in-law, who dropped me off right at the door, and the beauty in the kind employees who let us in early because it was 18 degrees outside. And the beauty in how the bookstore was so warm and cozy and the event was so well organized and calm. And the beauty of delicious coffee brewing in the air, and nice bathrooms. And the beauty of "Born to Run" erupting from the speakers every so often, whipping up the crowd, and the local news crews walking around interviewing people. And the beauty in meeting the two guys standing behind me and talking to them for hours about all sorts of things, including how we all loved "The Boss."

So see, by the time I had my beautiful moment with Bruce Springsteen, I had already experienced dozens and dozens of smaller wonderful moments related to the event. It had truly been an amazing morning before I had even said hello, shaken his hand, and posed for a picture (which, of course, was as big a moment as they come).

In the end, it was an incredible day, and it continued to be long into the night as I told my story to family and friends. And there was even more beauty a month later at Christmas, when my husband got my picture with Bruce made into a poster and a coffee mug that illuminated the photo when hot liquid was poured in.

So the next time you're in one of those big moments, like your daughter's wedding or a new baby arriving or buying your first house, think about all those other beautiful moments that are supporting it.

Because you'll see them sparkling there if you just look a little bit closer.

Today's Assignment:

1. Set your morning intention.
2. See those beautiful moments today and enter them in your journal.

Extra Credit: Those Smaller Moments

Think back on a time when you had one of those big moments of beauty. It could be anything as long as it was big for you. Write a few lines about the beauty of that event and then go a little bit deeper by writing down some more about those smaller moments that were surrounding it. Give yourself enough time to think through this exercise, listing as many moments as possible.

DAY 11: LOOKING FOR BEAUTY

Jesus replied, 'The kingdom of Heaven is spread upon the earth but men do not see it.'

The Gospel of Thomas

As I hope you are discovering, beauty is everywhere.

And you've probably also realized that it's not just about seeing beauty, but also about touching it, tasting it, smelling it, hearing it. *Feeling* it.

So remember to use all your senses when you're looking for beauty. Go wide and be free. Push yourself even further than those flowers and animals and faces that you've been drawing. Embrace the smells, voices, music, feelings, whispers, and every other point of beauty that surrounds you.

Here are a few ideas to help you expand on your journal entries:

- What kind of beauty have you touched recently? (Soft skin, your cat's fur, powdery snow that you brushed off your mailbox, bread dough at your fingertips, warm sheets fresh out of the dryer.)
- What kind of beauty have you tasted recently? (A cheesy delicious quesadilla with fresh guacamole, a sparkling

lime water, pumpkin pie with bourbon whipped cream, a passionate kiss.)

• What kind of beauty have you smelled recently? (Piñon burning in the fireplace, cookies baking in the oven, the roses you passed by as you entered the grocery store.)

• What kind of beauty have you heard recently? (The War on Drugs song with that guitar solo that you can't get out of your head, the sound of the wind, the narrator's expressive voice on the audiobook you listened to before falling asleep, the way the toddler in the produce section said the word *asparagus*.)

• What kind of beauty have you felt recently? (A poem that moved you, the feeling when you love someone, the way watching your dog sleep makes you feel inside, the sweet relief when you have finally completed a big project at school or filed your taxes, beating the deadline by mere minutes.)

Using all your senses as you search for beauty will deepen your experience.

Today's Assignment:

1. Set your morning intention.
2. *See* beauty in your day, including at least one example from each of the five senses.

Extra Credit: 10 Points

In your journal list 10 points of beauty from each of your five senses that you've experienced recently.

DAY 12: MARATHON

Don't quit. Suffer now and live the rest of your life as a champion.
Muhammed Ali

A few years back I decided to walk a marathon.

It was a huge decision for a lot of reasons, mostly because doing something like a marathon really isn't my thing. I'm not an athlete by any means. Some people, like my husband, eat marathons for breakfast. Me, I carry around extra weight and read in bed under a heavy down comforter on Sunday afternoons.

So why did I sign up for the Portland Marathon? I guess the bottom line was that I just wanted to see if I could do it. And I was happy when I crossed the finish line, having learned a few things along the way.

Like the importance of good-fitting shoes. And not over-dressing despite the rain. And drinking enough water to stay hydrated, even if you're not feeling thirsty. And how you really have to go at your own pace, not the pace of the people around you, or you could burn out in the first five miles with 21.2 still to go.

But probably the most important thing I learned was that my success was all about habits. Finishing was made possible by showing up every day to the training for three months before the race. It was about me walking around the college track, trekking city sidewalks, hiking mountain trails. About tying up my laces even when all I really wanted to do was crawl back in bed with a good book.

Showing up every day for a walking practice was both the easiest and hardest thing in the world. Easy because it was basic, putting one foot in front of the other and keeping track of miles. But hard because I had to do it consistently, no matter the weather outside or my mood inside.

But by sticking to it, a huge shift took place. I started feeling like an athlete for the first time in my life, and that ultimately helped me cross that finish line.

Creating that daily routine was how I got that medal around my neck and a silver space blanket over my shoulders.

Of course, all of this reminds me of the daily practice of seeing beauty. Because that's all we're doing here in this program: forming the habit of looking for beauty every day. And if you're able to do that, you'll also experience that shift inside, a shift that will allow you to regularly see what an amazing world you live in.

And that's a habit worth fighting for.

Today's Assignment:

1. Set your morning intention of seeing the beauty in your day.
2. Record the beauty later in your journal.

Extra Credit: Habits

Think about some of the daily habits you have in your life right now. Write about them in your journal, addressing the following:

• List all the activities that you do every single day (brushing your teeth, exercising, eating more kale).
• How were you successful in creating a daily routine for those activities? What motivates you to continue?

- Are there some habits that you've abandoned? Why did you stop doing them?
- How can you apply the success of your daily habits to the *See the Beauty* program?

DAY 13: FRESH EYES

When your eyes are tired
the world is tired also.
When your vision has gone,
no part of the world can find you.

David Whyte

Seeing the world in a different light happens once in a while on its own, but not too often. It's usually after something traumatic, like when you've landed on solid ground after a white-knuckle, turbulent flight, or when you've reached the end of a 24-hour vomit-and-diarrhea spree following a bout with norovirus. You're usually so thankful for being alive afterward that you can see all the sparkling beauty around you. Beauty that a day before you probably wouldn't have even noticed.

When you have this heightened sense of love and appreciation for your life, you're seeing the world with fresh eyes. Which is why one day back when I was teaching, I took a walk out to the playground with 32 fourth graders. They hadn't had a horrible stomach flu or anything like that, but my intent was to get them to see something new in something old. The playground would be the perfect place.

"We're heading outside!" I said right after the morning announcements. "We're going on a walk. Bring your poetry journals and pencils."

When they settled down, I continued.

"There are two rules, however. First, no talking. Or at least, not much. Can you do that?"

Most nodded.

I explained that poets must be quiet so they can pay attention to what's in front of them and write about it.

"The second rule is to notice everything."

"Like a fart?" Jon said.

"Exactly," I said. "But leave out names."

The students laughed. I could tell that they were more than a little excited about going out to the playground during *forbidden* hours. And to my surprise, they took the "be like a poet" assignment seriously, quickly putting on their coats and quietly lining up.

We walked past classrooms full of other students working at desks and then pushed through the double steel doors. We marched around the building, past the bungalows and the soccer field, past the bright blue play equipment. Noisy crows flew overhead, ducking into a grove of tall pine trees. A chilly breeze blew into our faces. We made our way over to the short wall near the basketball hoops and took a seat. They looked around. Some kids opened their journals and started writing.

The custodian suddenly appeared, dragging a yellow trash can across the yard and then stopped abruptly, staring at us. A few of the children waved, and she waved back. A few scribbled. The wind pushed swings into the metal poles, filling the air with a melodic chime. More pencils moved across the page.

Sarah jumped down from the wall and walked over to the grass, which was coated in a thin frost. She touched it and then wrote. Garrett followed and did the same thing. Kids watched, and as I walked around checking their progress, I noticed that some had written about their two classmates touching white grass with red fingers.

"Remember to use all your senses. Does anyone smell anything?"

"I smell cold," someone said.

"Write that down."

It was sublime, being out there with them in that moment as they saw the beauty of the quiet playground, watching them all slow down and really take the time to notice.

When we returned to the warm classroom, I told them to sit quietly at their desks, think, and write down some more notes. Then we gathered together to share our observations.

Adam had noticed the crows, and then said that they were probably hanging around waiting for lunch. Lisa talked about how quiet the playground was, how usually it's so loud with kids playing and whistles blowing. Landry said he saw a Twix wrapper blowing across the yard. Shannon mentioned how the janitor stared at us for a long time like she was wondering what we were doing out there. And shy Alex who rarely shared, told us about the dog in a car that passed by on the street beyond the field.

Before I set them loose to write their poems, I reminded them again about how poets open their hearts and drink in the sorrows and the beauty of the world. I told them how special it was, what they had done, taking the time to notice all the things around them. How most people don't bother. They walk past so many interesting things because they're busy thinking about something else.

What I didn't tell them back then, and what I wish I had, was this: As you get older, make a point of being a poet in your own life and always take the time to see the beauty in your world.

Because if you can do that, your life will be magical.

Today's Assignment:

1. Set your morning intention.
2. Notice the beauty during your day and record it in your journal.

Extra Credit: Be a Poet

Be a poet in your own life today. Notice everything. Take a few extra minutes noticing the things you usually ignore. Expand your world, soak it all in.

DAY 14: HARD DAYS

The way a crow
Shook down on me
The dust of snow
From a hemlock tree

Has given my heart
A change of mood
And saved some part
Of a day I had rued.

Robert Frost
"Dust of Snow"

Some days are hard. Some days are really hard. And when a strong feeling of doom swamps over you like a rogue wave in the blackest of nights, sometimes it's impossible to see the beauty.

And that's okay.

We experience life in ebbs and flows, see both valleys and peaks, live through the good and bad. So don't be hard on yourself if you're standing in a place where you can't see anything but the hard stuff in life. Ride it out the best you can. Tomorrow is another day.

But it's good to remember this in those times: Even during the worst of days, there might be a beautiful sunrise, mist floating up through the trees, seagulls squawking above, a soft breeze cooling you off. Even when you're feeling horribly sad, there could be a kind hospice nurse taking care of your mother, your big orange cat meowing happily when you step through the door, dinner waiting for you on the table. Even when you've cried all day, there could be a warm bed, your favorite music, a cherished book on the nightstand.

See the Beauty isn't about pretending everything is great during those times you feel disheartened and shattered. It's about opening your red, swollen eyes when you start to feel just a little bit better and letting the good come back into focus.

As you move through your life actively seeking out beauty, even on hard days, the beauty you find will comfort you. And as it comforts you, your heart will expand and slowly heal.

Today's Assignment:

1. Set your morning intention.
2. See the beauty in your day and record it later in your journal.

Extra Credit: Thinking Back

Think back to a particularly hard period in your life. Write a little bit about it in your journal, making sure to answer the following questions:

- Now that you've had some time to reflect, were there any moments of beauty that you might not have noticed during that tough time?
- Did you learn anything after going through that challenging event?
- Did you learn something that you can use in the future?

DAY 15: THE BEAUTY OF CREATIVITY

We did not ask for this room or this music; we were invited in. There-fore, because the dark surrounds us, let us turn our faces toward the light. Let us endure hardship to be grateful for plenty...We did not ask for this room or this music. But because we are here, let us dance.

Stephen King

There are a lot of steps in writing a novel, but I've found that the most important one is letting go so that the universe can work its magic. But before that can happen, I have to go through a little hell.

No matter how many books I've written, it's always brutal in the beginning. It's hard to sit down and begin chasing a story when nothing is speaking to me. Sure, I'll have a few ideas and some lines, but it only takes 10 minutes to type those out. The rest of the time is spent staring at the blank computer screen, at the walls, out the window, at the laundry piled in the corner, at my cat. And because writing is how I make my living, if this period lasts too long and those unproductive hours tick by, doubts and worries roll in like a storm.

But at least now I know that if I stick with it, eventually the next step will kick in.

But, truthfully, that step is even worse.

At this point the words are pouring from my brain and onto the page. And while some of the ideas are decent, most of the writing is pretty bad. So bad, I wouldn't even share it with my cat (although he is always very encouraging, reminding me to push through the mucky muck).

It's in the next step when I finally get some relief.

This is when I'm in the flow and my words have more depth and rhythm. I'm on the heels of something now, a story that needs to be told. I'm running hard after it, which basically means I'm showing up to my computer for hours each day. It is soon after this that something amazing often happens.

I'm allowed inside a wondrous place where instead of chasing the story, it starts chasing me.

It gives me ideas about what I should add, what's missing. It shows me scenes, lets me hear the voices of my characters, and has me feel the conflict and pain. It guides me toward plotlines and twists. The story now talks to me all the time: in the shower, in line at the grocery store, before I fall asleep at night.

This is my favorite part of the creative process. I don't know what it is exactly, God, a muse, my own higher power. Whatever it is, something spiritual seems to be offering a helping hand. In these moments the story knows much more than I do and tells me things that I wouldn't have thought of on my own.

Sometimes it only takes a minute to see the magic, but other times it takes years.

Take *Forty-Four* for example, the title of my first series.

When the thought came to me to call the first book a number, I had no idea why or what it meant. All I knew at the time was that I had been writing about a teenager, Abby Craig, who lived in Bend, Oregon, and who drowned one winter afternoon, but then woke up from death. When the title idea was first whispered in my ear, I liked the sound of "Forty-Four" and thought it was compelling. But then I had to figure out how to apply it to Abby and her story.

I did some research on near-death experiences and discovered that some drowning victims started breathing again and lived to tell their tale. Some had been *dead* for more than an hour. I decided that it would fit, that Abby Craig had been dead for 44 minutes. It seemed perfect and I went ahead with it, not only using the title for the first book, but for the entire 13-book series.

But a few years later I found out something else.

The latitude coordinate for Bend, where the story takes place, is *44*.05643.

Wild.

Another example of this magic involves *Book Eleven*. Abby is on the run, wanted for a murder she didn't commit, and ends up in Hatch, New Mexico. I didn't know anything about the small town other than what I had read online, basically that it was a place where chiles were grown and harvested. I learned about migrant workers who took a bus from El Paso at three in the morning to arrive at the fields before dawn, and how they worked until sundown.

It was the exact place Abby needed to be: desolate and harsh, an area rich with sad stories and brutal conditions. A place where her tears would blend in with all the others, a place that would either push her over the edge or closer to finding her strength and power.

I finished writing *Book Eleven*, published it, and moved on to the next. But a few summers later, when I was driving with my husband through New Mexico, I made a startling discovery.

As we got closer to the small town of Hatch, there on Highway 180, I started noticing the mile marker posts.

"This is kind of weird," I said as we sped down the road. "I think Hatch is going to be pretty close to mile 44."

"Really?"

"Yeah, look."

And sure enough, as we passed milepost 44, a giant water tower up on a hill came into view. A water tower with writing on it: *Welcome to Hatch!*

"That's crazy," I said. "We gotta stop."

Joe pulled off so I could take some photos. It was so hard to believe. Hatch began at the 44th mile.

A few minutes later, merging onto Interstate 25, it happened again.

On a completely different highway, just as we passed by the very last chile field on our way out of town, there was yet another "44" milepost sign.

Although these things can give me the chills, they also leave me in a state of awe and deep thankfulness. It's astonishing and humbling to realize that my writing is sometimes touched by magic.

And the best part is that this creative energy is available to everyone. All you need to do is be willing to put in the blood, sweat, and tears so you can get your ticket in.

Today's Assignment:

1. Set your morning intention.
2. See the beauty in your day and capture those moments in your journal.

Extra Credit: Crossing Over

Have you had any experience or interaction with the creative process? If so, write or draw about it in your journal. If not, would you like to? To unlock the magic choose something that you like doing (painting, writing, drawing, sculpting, knitting, singing, running, dancing) and start spending a lot of time doing it. Commit to going to a deeper level and you'll find your muse.

DAY 16: GET BACK ON THE HORSE

Rivers know this: There is no hurry. We shall get there someday.
                                                              A.A. Milne
                                                       Winnie-the-Pooh

You thought it was a good idea at the time.

You bought and began reading this book, got a new journal, set lots of morning intentions, and even started using those brand new colored pencils. And maybe too you had a few really great weeks of seeing the beauty in your life.

But...

Wednesday you worked late. Thursday you were too sick to reach for anything except NyQuil and the TV remote. By Sunday you weren't just off the boat, you couldn't even see the water anymore.

So what to do if you fall behind in the 30-day program?

Easy.

Just pick up a pencil and start again, from wherever you are.

Life happens and sometimes even our best intentions can get derailed. But in the big picture, there is no being off track because there is no track. You are free to wander in a million different directions. You are free to stop. And you are free to get back into the program.

There have been days when I've missed doing my entries, and there's even been a few dark days when I've absolutely refused to open my journal. But even with those occasional bumps in the road, over the years I've still collected stacks of completed journals. And the reason is simple. I always come back to the practice because I know how important it is. Long ago, when I began the habit of reflecting on all the beauty of my day, something resonated so deep inside that even now when I don't get to my journal, it feels strange.

One trick that helps is this: On those days when I don't feel like I have the time to sit and color and think and write, I cut the time commitment to five minutes instead of twenty. I write down short phrases all across the blank page (I can even do this as I'm making dinner). And when I do have more time later in the week I'll go back and add the drawings. This way no matter what, I've made note of those special moments.

If you've been at it every day, bravo! Keep it going, keep capturing all the beautiful moments in your life. But if you've fallen off the horse, just… Oh, hell, you know what to do.

Today's Assignment:

1. Set your morning intention.
2. See the beauty in your day and record it later in your journal.

Extra Credit: Right Now

From where you are, look around you and notice the beauty. Don't write about it or illustrate it, just spend a few moments right now appreciating it.

DAY 17: THE BEAUTY IN PETS

Ask the beasts and they will teach you the beauty of this earth.
Saint Francis of Assisi

A few months after we moved to the Arizona desert, one of those violent storms blew in signaling the beginning of the monsoon season. It was a wild and big event, with torrential rain, fierce winds, apocalyptic thunder, and long, jagged lightning bolts streaking across the black sky. It was straight out of one of those old haunted house movies. Or the kind written about in the Old Testament, that forces you to stop and think about what it means to be alive—and staying alive as well.

When the rain first started pummeling the roof, I jumped up from the sofa and followed my family outside to watch the show from beneath the covered patio. Dewey, my daughter's 90-pound puppy, pushed out ahead of us at full speed, excited to experience his first-ever monsoon. The thunder roared above us, but he seemed to love it. He began dancing, turning, twisting, and circling around, a joy radiating from him as real as the pink tongue flapping from the side of his mouth. He did his famous 360-degree turns on his butt, running back and forth and back again. He stayed out there in that hard rain for a long, long time.

Dew seemed to love everything about the chaos of the weather. The water pooling on top of the parched soil before turning into a raging river. The sound the raindrops made on the tin roof. The violence of the thunder. The bright streaks lighting up the saguaros and everything else around us.

As I watched his joy, I couldn't help but think that the puppy had the right idea. I wondered if it was possible to train myself to approach new and different things the same way Dewey approached the monsoon. I wondered if I could learn to embrace change, instead of overthinking it. If I could somehow find a way to dance more and worry less, if I could breathe in the electricity of the new instead of shuddering in fear of the unknown.

It still makes me smile, even today, the thought of him out there in the rain. And it always reminds me how sometimes our four-legged friends are really quite beautiful in the way they can deliver a message.

Today's Assignment:

1. Set your morning intention.
2. See the beauty in your day and record it in your journal later.

Extra Credit: Pets!

Have you experienced the beauty of the animal kingdom? If so, spend some time writing about a favorite memory or two of a pet or an animal you've observed (your cat kneading the blanket at your feet, a crow hopping around, a coyote strolling down a suburban street at dusk like he owned it). When you're done add in some illustrations and color.

DAY 18: THE BEAUTY OF DISSOLVING DREAMS

The best way to make your dreams come true is to wake up.

Paul Valery

For years I dreamed of being a writer. It started early, back in first grade when I wrote a short story about a dragon, and it lasted all the way up until my mid-forties.

But although I longed and ached to be a writer, the idea of *being* one felt impossible. Writers were holy. They had the ability to create other worlds, to make people feel and think. I wasn't worthy.

Even in those fleeting moments when I dared to think that maybe, just maybe, I had what it took, I had no idea how to go about making it a career. I'd write a few short stories every once in a while and submit them for publication, but they almost always came back with a "thanks, but no thanks."

Those notes caused more than a few tears, but they didn't stop the dream. In fact they only fueled my obsession. I devoured books on writing, read about famous authors and their writing routines, attended writing conferences, and watched movies about writers and those people like me who wanted to be writers.

I wondered how all those published authors got their jobs, their big breaks. Were they just lucky so-and-sos? Were they born with silver quills in their hands, raised in East Coast families that had all the right connections? It was a frustrating mystery.

I even tried doing some visualization of signing book contracts and going to those fancy parties with salty hors d'oeuvres and champagne served in handcrafted crystal flutes. It was all great!

All I needed was to be called up to the big leagues, and *then* I would begin writing my great American novel. I was ready, except for one little thing.

The writing.

Over the years I hadn't done too much of it.

Then, one day something strange happened. I was talking with my youngest daughter, who had recently graduated from college, when out of the blue she suggested something wild and crazy.

"Why don't you write a book?"

I paused, feeling a little breathless.

"What do you mean?"

"I mean, you know that thing you've been talking about since I was little? Why not just finally write that book?"

My daughter was one smart cookie. She was suggesting that instead of thinking about writing a book or reading about writing a book or attending events about how to write a book or watching movies about writing a book, that I should just sit down and write a book!

"Hmmmmm," I said, feeling that familiar tightness in my throat. "I guess I could try."

And that was how the dream dissolved and began becoming a reality.

After that, I took writing seriously, which meant I started spending hours each day at the computer. The hours turned into weeks and the weeks into months and then finally into a book. I repeated the process over and over and over again until one day I found myself with a 13-volume series.

Within a few years of dissolving my dream I was not only telling people that I was a writer without breaking out into a sweat, but I also had to tell the IRS that I was a writer (which did make me break out in a sweat).

The obsessive dreaming and little doing I had done for de-cades had kept me from being a writer. Now the path seems simple and logical, if not easy. I start in the morning with a blank page, work on characters and plots and dialogue, and at the end of the day I can call myself a writer.

Everything else floating around the profession is dust in the wind. Writing is what makes me a writer.

Dreams are beautiful and necessary, but they're only a be-ginning. I learned that transforming a dream into reality takes changing your mindset and doing the work. Do the work and you will become what it is you're dreaming about. Demystifying the dream makes it attainable and real.

I don't get all choked up over the idea of being a writer anymore. I never have a lump in my throat or goosebumps down my arms when I turn off my computer and call it a day. Most of the time I get up from my desk, change the laundry, go through the mail, and get some dinner.

But every once in a while I will drink champagne from a handcrafted crystal flute.

Today's Assignment:

1. Set your morning intention.
2. See the beauty and render it in your journal later in the day or night, making sure to add art and background colors.

Extra Credit: Dreams

Do a little dream analysis on yourself, answering the fol-lowing questions:

• What dreams did you have when you were young?
• What dreams have you been able to turn into reality?
• What were some of the strategies you used for turning a dream into reality?
• What dreams do you have now?
• What are some strategies you could use to make them come true?

DAY 19: THE BEAUTY OF SELFISHNESS

I got my own back.

Maya Angelou

As I mentioned in an earlier essay, I'm a huge Bruce Springsteen fan. And as I also mentioned, there were countless beautiful moments connected to meeting him.

But I forgot one of the most important ones.

It had been a great morning, a morning filled with anticipation, meeting new friends, and standing in line with an excited crowd. The hours had flown by and then, suddenly, at about 11:30 an announcement was made.

"Listen up, everybody! Bruce has 1000 people to see today, so here is the plan. You'll give your camera to one of our employees and they will take your picture with him. You can't wait or linger after your photo is taken because it will clog up the line and slow things down. You must move along."

My heart pounded in my chest while a crazy smile took hold of my face (one that wouldn't disappear for the next 24 hours). A few minutes later people at the front of the line started cheering.

He had arrived.

I couldn't help but notice that the two women in front of me were looking a little upset. I had attempted more than once to strike up a conversation during our nearly four-hour wait to-gether but didn't have much luck. They had kept to themselves, talked in whispers and ignored not just me, but everyone around them (except the news reporters and cameramen). They gave off that same nasty vibe as those snobby girls in middle school from so long ago. But they were an anomaly in a vast sea of happy fans.

As I took a step closer toward the black curtain that hid Bruce from the crowd, one of the women suddenly turned around and looked at me.

"I have a favor to ask," she said.

In my gleeful state, any request by anybody would probably have been fine. I mean, I was meeting Bruce Springsteen in just a few minutes. Life was amazing!

"Sure," I said. "What do you need?"

"Well, it's a pay-it-forward favor, something someone will do for you some day."

I stood there trying to decipher her words, but it was of course impossible since she had missed the entire concept of "paying it forward" by about 10 miles. I began to ask her exactly what she needed when the people ahead of us once again began screaming. Bright flashes lit up the room like fireworks.

"See, my friend here is going to meet him first, and I'm go-ing to take her picture."

She held up a small camera as if to prove her point. But I was still confused.

"You don't need to take any pictures, the bookstore employ-ees will be doing that," I said, craning my neck sideways to try and get a peek at Bruce through the crack in the curtains.

She sighed. The middle-aged middle schooler was getting frustrated.

"Yes," she said, "but we want *extra* pictures, in case we don't like the ones they take. We each brought another camera in ad-dition to our phones."

I could see the people up ahead now breaking into huge star-struck grins as they turned the corner.

"So, anyway, I'll be able to take my friend's picture, but she won't be able to take mine because she can't wait on the other side. That's the favor. I need you to take *my* picture."

We inched up and turned the corner and lo and behold, Bruce was up ahead, his arm wrapped around someone's shoulder, both of them smiling. It was him! He was really here! And I was really going to meet him in a few minutes. What would I say? How would I say it? Would I even be able to speak?

"So," the woman said. "Do you mind?"

I took in a breath, thought about it, and realized that I actually did mind.

It had taken so much to get to this spot. I needed to center my thoughts, figure out what I was going to say, and calm down so that I didn't come across as a mute jack-o-lantern.

But saying no is not something I usually do, or something that I do easily. I really hate hurting people's feelings. Most of the time I'll just say yes, doing things I don't want to do, and regret it later. Like the time I lugged a five-ton suitcase over cobblestone streets and then up six flights of stairs because an acquaintance had asked me to so she could go to dinner.

But this time as I stood in line to meet Bruce Springsteen, I felt different. Inside. I guess it was all that excitement that helped me break free from my usual behavior and express exactly how I felt.

"No," I said. "Sorry. I can't. I really need to focus on the moment."

I could see that she was stunned, my words slapping her in the face. She sighed before turning back to her friend, resuming one of those whisper sessions they had been engaged in all morning.

But unlike back in middle school, I didn't care.

I was so in tune with everything around me, how I was about to have a magnificent moment with my rock hero, that all I cared about was walking over to Bruce, saying hello, and looking into his eyes.

Much later that night, as I was thinking about it, I was proud of myself for not having compromised my experience. I knew that if I had said yes and taken the picture, the moment would have bled away. I would have been worried about getting a good picture for her, and using her camera, and making sure that I found her outside so that I could return it, and having her camera in my hand for my own picture. If I had said yes, I would have traded in my own magical meeting with Bruce for a flustered and stressed shared experience with a greedy stranger.

That day I learned that "no" can be the most wonderful word in the dictionary. It was a glorious moment, a true selfish act.

And it was beautiful.

Today's Assignment:

1. Set your morning intention.
2. See the beauty in your day and record it later in your journal.

Extra Credit: Saying No

For many people, women especially, saying no is a hard thing to do. Along with our innate sense of compassion and caring, many of us have also been raised to be people pleasers, which makes it difficult when it comes to putting our own needs first.

But saying no to the things you don't want to do is really about taking care of yourself. And I can attest that it is never too late for that, never too late to learn.

So for today, write a little bit about saying no in your journal, making sure to express your thoughts and feelings on the idea of you rejecting something as well as answering the following questions:

- How does saying no usually make you feel? Guilty? Happy? Full of angst? Scared?
- When was the last time you said no to something that you didn't want to do? When was the last time you said yes to something you didn't want to do?
- How does not saying no (i.e., saying, "Yes, sure, whatever you need") make you feel when you really don't want to do something?
- Do you think that learning how to say no would be beneficial? If so, how would learning that new skill change your life? What would you do less of and what would you have more time for?

DAY 20: KEEP LOOKING

Turn your face toward the sun and the shadows will fall behind you.
Maori Proverb

If you're still here, take a moment and give yourself a pat on the back. You're way past the halfway point and you're doing great!

If you missed a few days or have ditched the morning intention or rushed through the journal exercises barely paying attention, don't beat yourself up over it. Forming a daily habit takes time. It's all about a series of baby steps, not one giant leap. It's a marathon, not a sprint. So if you haven't been consistent about your journal entries or morning intentions, it's a brand new day.

And if you're looking for new and different points of beauty, here are some more ideas:

Beauty is in the food that nourishes you, tantalizing your taste buds.

Beauty is in those "firsts" that make you feel amazing, like meeting someone new or going to a new city for the very first time.

Beauty is in those things that lift your spirits like singing or running or creating art.

Beauty is in the soft afternoon light that brightens the winter-dead branches on a tree.

Beauty is in that good morning kiss.

Beauty is in the poem that you read on the train ride to work.

Beauty is in meeting your hero.

Beauty is in being your own hero.

Beauty is in that PR you just set.

Beauty is in getting through the speech.

Beauty is in lighting candles.

Beauty is in that new idea that gets you pumped up.

Beauty is when you love your life.

Today's Assignment:

1. Set your morning intention.
2. See the beauty in your day and record it in your journal later.

Extra Credit: Mindful Eating

Be present during an entire meal. The next meal you sit down to eat, make an effort to be as present as possible. Even if there are other people around, make it a point to focus on what you're eating. What does the food taste like? Can you detect subtle flavors that you didn't before? Try to clear your mind and focus your entire attention on every aspect of the meal. Chew slowly, savoring every bite. When your mind starts to wander, gently direct it back to the present moment.

DAY 21: THE BEAUTY OF YOU

Be humble, for you are made of earth. Be noble, for you are made of stars.

Serbian Proverb

You. Are. Beautiful.

Maybe you don't hear that anymore, or maybe you don't hear it enough, or maybe you've never heard it. And maybe reading this right now makes you feel uncomfortable, stirring something inside that makes you want to argue.

But I'll write it again: You are beautiful.

There is no one on this planet like you. No one with your exact combination of... *you.* Nobody with the precise mixture of your straight hair, curly toes, and dimples, with your height and weight and eye color and round face and wide crooked-tooth smile that erupts when you're truly happy inside. With your thoughts, beliefs, ideas, and dreams. Someone who likes to make wishes on full moons, picks huckleberries for summer pies, cries during opera arias. Someone with both Jack White and Beethoven on the same playlist.

So far, this program has been about bringing into focus the beauty that surrounds your life. But now it's time for you to see and realize how magnificent *you* are.

It's not always easy to do, not in a sales-driven, superficial society that tries to make you feel inadequate, tries to convince you that you are not enough, that you need something else, that beauty is only reserved for the lucky few.

But it's time for you to look past what they're trying to sell and see how wonderful you are.

You are your own beautiful hero on a beautiful journey.

Today's Assignment:

1. Set your morning intention.
2. Record the beauty in your journal later in the day. Add in at least three points of beauty that you noticed about yourself today.

Extra Credit: I Am Poem

Writing poetry can be fun and working on this "I Am" poem can also be a great learning experience. Choose from the lines below to complete your poem. You don't have to use all of them. Fill in personal details as you go and be creative with your answers, thinking outside the box.

Copy the finished product into your *See the Beauty* journal. Add some color and a few illustrations. Celebrate the beautiful you!

"I Am" Poem

I am... (your name)
I love... (list at least one thing)
I know... (list at least one thing)
I believe... (list at least one thing)
I wish... (list at least one thing)
I want... (list at least one thing)
I'm excited when... (list at least one thing)
I'm happiest when... (list at least one thing)
I dream about... (list at least one thing)
I love learning about... (list at least one thing)

I love going to…. (list at least one thing)
I love creating… (list at least one thing)
I love hearing… (list at least one thing)
I love seeing… (list at least one thing)
I love feeling… (list at least one thing)
I love touching… (list at least one thing)
I love smelling… (list at least one thing)
I am… (name)

Example:

Jools

I love long road trips through the desert, first snows, sparkling swimming pools, novels about stolen art and WWII, ocean waves pounding the shore, sitting by a bonfire, hanging out with family and friends.

I know how to paddle on the Green River, how to write a book, the storylines of five operas, how to make gnocchi while surrounded in clouds of flour dust.

I believe in the magic of the Universe.

I wish for inner peace, more trips back home to Bend, a Pad Thai recipe that knocks my socks off, to sit in restaurants overlooking the Amalfi Coast.

I'm excited when the Dodgers win, when the World Cup begins, for Sunday night dinners, packing for a trip and also returning home.

I'm happiest when writing, eating good food, drinking good wine, hiking in red rock country, cooking, when my toes are in the sand.

I dream about tropical islands, Florence, hitting number one on the NYT Bestseller list.

Jools

DAY 22: THE BEAUTY IN BAD JOBS

Ultimately there is no such thing as failure. There are lessons learned in different ways.

Twyla Tharp

When our kids were little, my husband and I sacrificed, struggled, and pieced things together so that I could be a stay-at-home mom for nearly 10 years. I loved being home, taking care of our two daughters. It was good and important work, and I knew that I was lucky to be able to do it.

But when the time came to get a job, I was stumped. Back in college, working long hours on the school newspaper, I figured I was on track for a career in journalism. And while I had sold a few articles over the years, it was for very little money. My successes felt very far away, barely visible in the rearview mirror of my mind's eye. And they felt very small. It left me feeling like getting a job outside of the home was worlds away, out of reach. Sure, I was good at writing stories and I was good at herding a band of second graders through museum field trips, but who was going to pay me for those things?

By the time my two daughters were at the tail end of elementary school, my confidence had fallen below sea level. I wasn't that great on a computer and I absolutely had no references other than a bunch of thumbs up from the various kids I encountered throughout my day.

The more I dwelled in this negative space, the more I really believed that I'd never find a job, that I was basically unemployable. But to my surprise, a few months after my oldest went into the sixth grade, a job opportunity came flying toward me like a cannonball. A friend told me that the place where she worked was hiring and she could get me in. It didn't pay much, she said, but the boss was really nice and the shifts were in the mornings, which would be perfect.

Kelly answered the phones and set appointments, but I wouldn't be doing that. I wasn't exactly sure what I'd be doing, but I was intrigued by the ease of it all. I went ahead and called Daryl, the owner.

"You can start on Monday," he said. "Wear comfortable clothes."

I found out that I'd be working at an auto detailing business, and when I arrived and was shown all the spray bottles and rags, I quickly realized that "detailing" meant cleaning. Daryl took me into a bay on a drizzly, gray morning, pointing to the cleansers and polishers I'd use, the vacuum hanging down from the ceiling, the trash bins lined against the back wall. I then met Zac, a tall, hefty, 20-year-old with curly hair and glasses who did the job full-time. He said hello and then flipped on a switch that sent Top 40 radio vibrating throughout the garage. We got to work.

Hours turned into days and days turned into weeks, weeks of collecting and tossing out old fast food wrappers, stiff gas station receipts, paper bags, smashed Big Gulp cups, napkins and tissues and leaves and wires, crumpled soda cans, and broken plastic utensils. I sprayed dashboards and seats and steering wheels, vacuumed carpets, squeegeed windows, washed out smelly ashtrays, wiped down doors and handles, and emptied glove boxes all while "No Diggity" blasted in the background every hour on the hour.

I was filthy and wet each morning within the first few minutes and shivering the rest of the time in the cold Oregon autumn. Grime and grease and dirt caked onto my body and soul.

I'd spray and spray and spray, forced to listen to the non-stop chatter of the manboy next to me who was in love with comic books, only stopping his monologue when Blackstreet and Dr. Dre came on so that he could sing along.

Hours. Crawled. By.

I would drive home exhausted, my hands and fingers aching, my mind numb, my lungs full of chemical-rich phlegm. I knew the job wasn't working, wasn't good for me in so many ways, and as I pulled into the driveway I'd promise myself that I'd quit. But for some strange reason by the time I fell into bed at night I was resigned to get up and do it all over again the next day.

I wish I could report that I soon saw the beauty in this job, that I suddenly saw a sweetness in Zac's non-stop babbling, or that a feeling of "wow" rushed over me when I gazed up at the clouds on my 10-minute break, but I'd be lying. I hated that damn job. Hated it with every cell of my being. Hated being with those people all morning, hated the damp filth, hated the smell of the antiseptic cleaners. And most of all, I hated the way it left me feeling.

Every night my husband would say, "Please, quit. Just quit. It's not worth it."

And every night I would tell him I couldn't quit because we needed the money. And then he pointed out that it wasn't really that much money. And I'd counter by saying, "Yeah, but it's something." And when he said that there were lots of better jobs out there, that's when I would freeze. I wouldn't say it out loud, but I was afraid that if I walked away from this job, this horrible job, I'd never be able to get another one.

Thankfully, I was just around the corner from a breakthrough.

A few days later an old blue pickup was waiting for me in the bay. I opened the creaky door on the passenger's side and started pulling trash from under the seat. I reached down and grabbed handfuls of leaves and twine, but jumped back when I saw that in my gloved hand there was also a huge dead rat.

"Eeew," I said, flinging it onto the floor.

Zac laughed and told me that it happened a lot, finding dead things in old cars.

I stood there and stared down at the dried-up corpse.

Miraculously, in that moment, my self-esteem rose up from the grave. It wasn't that I was particularly scared of deceased rodents, but something about that rat had finally shaken me out of my stupor and made me realize that I deserved better.

At the end of the week, I quit.

And not long after that, I pulled my head out of that dark place and got myself back to school. I enrolled in a master's program in education and a few years later landed a teaching job.

It was only much later that I was able to see that there really was beauty in that bad job.

Auto detailing helped me get where I wanted to go. It was a step along the way in my journey to a better place. But before I could move on, I needed to have a better vision of myself and for myself.

Another beautiful thing that came out of the experience is the running joke in my family that still makes us all laugh to this day. It involves a little pantomiming, holding a spray bottle and squeezing the trigger with one hand while wiping with the other, and singing the chorus from "No Diggity."

On my last day, I stopped in at the office to pick up my final check and say goodbye. Daryl wished me luck.

"Oh, and hey," he said, calling after me as I headed toward the door. "If you know any other moms who might need a job, let them know I'm hiring."

I smiled.

Today's Assignment:

1. Set your morning intention.
2. See the beauty in your day and record it later in your journal.

Extra Credit: Beauty in the Bad

Have you ever had an experience like the one described above? A bad job, a horrible relationship, a tough childhood? While all of these things are hardships, there are often gems beneath the surface of the experience if you take a little time to look.

Pick something that was difficult for you and think about it for a while. When you're ready, write a paragraph or two describing the bad points in your journal. Then, write about the lessons you learned and/or the beauty you found in that situation, making sure to answer the following questions:

- Did you eventually find some good in the bad?
- Was there any other beauty surrounding that event?
- Can you see that this might be a good story to reflect on from time to time, reminding yourself that there can be beauty in the difficult situations you now face?

Extra, Extra Credit: Get Artsy

Creating art is a great way to de-stress after a bad day at work, letting your worries evaporate for a little while. So today spend some time creating art. It can be any kind of art that makes you happy, from crocheting to painting to sewing to drawing. Here are a few "artsy" ideas that I love doing when I have a little time.

- *Charcoal Sketching…* Of all the art mediums, I find this one to be the most relaxing.
- *Alcohol Inks…* Alcohol inks can be found at most art and craft stores, as well as online. If you're not familiar with them, look up some examples on YouTube to see what they are about. They are very abstract and colorful and it's the kind of art that always turns out great no matter what you do.
- *Paper Marbling…* Paper marbling is one of my all-time favorite activities, although to do it the "old-fashioned" way, it takes a lot of time, preparation, and skill. But recently, I came across a product that makes it super simple. It's called *Easy Marble.*

DAY 23: WHEN YOUR SHIP COMES IN

Forget not that the earth delights to feel your bare feet and the winds long to play with your hair.

Khalil Gibran

When I sit down to write a new book, I can barely see any of it. And staring at that blank page, it's hard not to panic. Nothing is there but the smallest of ideas.

It feels like I'm standing at the edge of a dock looking out at the ocean and all I see is water. Then I notice a speck on the horizon. And although I'm hoping it's that ship I've been waiting for, I really can't be sure. In that nervous moment, my heart races and it's hard to catch my breath.

But if I keep focusing, something amazing happens.

That speck keeps getting larger and larger as it comes into full view.

Suddenly, it's not a small dot anymore. It's a huge ship—my ship—racing toward me. In other words, the more I look, the more I see.

The last book in the *Forty-Four* series was exactly like that. When I sat down to write that final volume, all I could "see" was that Abby Craig had to confront her enemy. It was hard not to feel anxious because that's all I had and I needed more. A lot more. And I needed it to be big.

But writing books has taught me something. If I stick with it, the story emerges. So that's what I did. I kept staring, allowing more and more details to come into view. After a little while, I saw that Abby was heading to the Florida Keys on her motorcycle, and I saw that she was worried about trusting Samael, her traveling companion. And I saw that she wouldn't find her nemesis for a while, but eventually they would meet, in the water. And then I saw something else: She'd have to say goodbye to an old friend.

Seeing the beauty in your world involves this very same idea. Sometimes, you have to give it time and you have to stay focused before you can see what you're seeking.

Because really, if you think about it, there are thousands of points of beauty in your day. Probably even more. And they're always there, all the time—when you're feeling strong and also right alongside you on those dark days.

The more you look, the more you see.

Today's Assignment:

1. Set your morning intention.
2. See the beauty of your day and record it later in your journal.

Extra Credit: 100 Points of Beauty

This is one of my favorite exercises. You will need some time to complete it, so if you're busy today, schedule this for later.

Make a list of 100 points of beauty that have happened in your life (so far). The list should include the big things, like getting your college degree or going to Paris or bringing home your new puppy, and little things, like smelling orange blossoms in the air for the first time on a spring evening in Tucson. Don't think too hard on one particular thing, just keep your pencil moving.

Make sure to number the list as you go and use just a few words or phrases for each item (no complete sentences necessary).

Two tips for success in this exercise:

• Before you start, make a thoughtful list of 10 important things you feel you *must* include, such as giving birth to your children or marrying your high school sweetheart. Include everything that might leave you feeling awful if you accidently left it off your *100 Points of Beauty* list. (Because, believe it or not, it's easy to do as you get going in this stream-of-consciousness exercise). So take the first few minutes at the beginning and include those large things so you can let your mind run wild on everything else.

• The second tip for this exercise is to make it fun! Put on some music and let your mind wander back into those great moments of beauty that you've had in your life. Add a glass of wine or sparkling soda, a lit candle. This is, after all, a celebration of your life.

DAY 24: THE BEAUTY IN LEARNING

There is divine beauty in learning.

Elie Wiesel

Back when I was teaching, the term "lifelong learner" became a popular concept in education. Principals wanted teachers to embrace the idea so that we could model an attitude of passionate, continuous learning for students. But the problem was that they expected us to get pumped up about curriculum mapping and classroom management and the latest technique for getting kids to do well on state tests. And while these things were probably important on some level, none of them sparked immense joy in me. And the things that did seem rather exciting, like figuring out a way to use a karaoke machine so that my fourth graders could rap their poetry, didn't excite my principal all that much.

Plus, to be honest, the idea of taking more classes made my skin crawl. The images that came back to me whenever I thought about learning were not pretty. Those long, dry lectures I had to sit through at the university, that frantic note-taking, the stress over math equations I was expected to memorize, and the autopilot regurgitation of facts that I always seemed to forget the second I handed in a final.

Lifelong learning? No, thank you. I had paid my dues, had my degrees, and had no desire to be trapped on some academic hamster wheel for the rest of my life.

Then while making a pizza from scratch one day—the dough under my palm, the aroma of olive oil filling my nose—I had an epiphany. I realized that when it came to the things that mattered to me, I loved being a lifelong learner.

With cooking it began back when I was a young teenager. One day I decided to make my parents a gourmet dinner for their anniversary.

Raised in a household where the microwave was king and ruled with an iron fist (along with those sweet 70's fashions), the lack of good food during my childhood had left me hungry. I knew there was a world beyond silver-tinned TV dinners, Hamburger Helper boxes, and dehydrated potato gratin mixes. I had seen it on PBS shows and on the covers of cookbooks that lined the shelves at the book store.

I walked over to the library, pulled down a copy of Julia Child's *The Art of French Cooking,* and sat for hours reading through recipes and taking notes. I decided on a chicken dish, *Poulet en Gelée,* went shopping for the ingredients, and had my mom buy some white wine. I made do with what I had (by then we were down to that microwave and a Crockpot) and somehow made it work. At six o'clock on the dot, dinner was served. It was a glowing success. (With a faraway look in her eye, my mom talked about the time she ate my "delicious French meal" until the day she died.)

I didn't know it at the time, but that afternoon I spent studying in the library was my very first cooking lesson. And even though I didn't get much of a chance to continue my studies during school, I was able to eventually return to serious cooking in my late 20s.

Over the years I've learned about deglazing and sautéing and searing and simmering and braising. I've learned about spices and ingredients and how the right mix can take you all over the world, how tomatillos and poblano peppers will transport you to Mexico, how ghee and garam masala will take you to India, how basil and pine nuts and olive oil will take you to Genoa.

I've devoured cookbooks by Alice Waters and Marcus Samuelsson and Rick Bayless. Nigella. Ina. I learned about the five "mother" sauces. I learned how to make crepes and quiches, creamy fondues and gratins, fluffy madeleines and macaroons with perfect "feet."

I read and studied and learned everything I could about cooking, all with great enthusiasm and excitement. I memorized recipes, and then practiced and practiced and practiced. For years. I'm still practicing! And even though I've never had a desire to become a professional chef, I still want to learn as much as I can. And I know too that there is no end, that there will always be some new recipe that I'll want to try.

It occurred to me not long after my petition to get that karaoke machine was turned down, that my experience with cooking was exactly what being a lifelong learner was all about: choosing a subject that you have an interest in, and going into it much deeper by learning all you can. It's about spending countless hours studying something without breaking a sweat or even looking at the clock.

Of course, there is a place for that other kind of learning, the formal one with all those heavy textbooks and tests. It is often the only way to get where you want to go.

But it's in that other realm, where your passion lives, that you'll find the true magic.

And the beauty of learning.

Today's Assignment:

1. Set your morning intention.
2. See the beauty in your day and spend time recording it in your journal later.

Extra Credit: Reflecting

Write a few paragraphs about your own learning experiences, making sure to touch on the following:

• List some of your favorite subjects in school. What did you love learning about? Are you still interested in those things and have you continued learning?

• Have you taken any classes recently that you love (painting, knitting, hip hop dancing, paddle boarding, web design, *See the Beauty*)?

• List the different things that you've learned this year. (Did you learn more about the game of baseball? Chiaroscuro? How to make a port and fig sauce?)

• Make a list of some of the things you would like to learn about in the coming year.

DAY 25: THE BEAUTY OF MUSIC

The world is full of magic things, patiently waiting for our senses to grow sharper.

W.B. Yeats

Recently I put together a playlist for my birthday. I started with current songs, but then added more and more "oldies" as I remembered music from my past. I was grateful that I had finished writing for the day because the list literally took hours to complete.

There was the Partridge Family, Cher, Peter Frampton, and the Bee Gees, which all represented my childhood. The Pretenders were there, taking me back to that day I walked to my favorite record store and saw that album cover of Chrissie Hynde holding a guitar and looking so badass (sold!). Blondie and Oingo Boingo were definitely on my list, along with Pat Benatar and the Motels and Bon Jovi. The Police was there. And Tom Petty, who reminded me of that first official date with Mr. Jools at the Universal Amphitheater, and how we fell in love that summer and everything was so magical. And, of course, I put lots of Bruce on the playlist.

The grunge years were represented by Nirvana and Pearl Jam and Alice in Chains, stirring memories of those trips we'd take up to Seattle to visit my in-laws. The Cure was there too, and it reminded me how Robert Smith is always so masterful at capturing sadness in his music. I added Chris Isaak, Prince, Lucinda Williams, the Replacements, Live, Van Morrison, Michael Jackson, U2, the Waterboys, Lyle Lovett, Kathleen Edwards, Beth Hart, Florence and the Machine, Amy Winehouse, War on Drugs, and Kings of Leon.

I included some of those high-intensity, not-usually-my-kind-of-music songs by Beyoncé and Justin Timberlake and Eminem and Sia because I love listening to them at the gym. I added in some Gardel, the Gypsy Kings, Diana Krall, Tony Bennett, Johnny Hartman, Melody Gardot, music I listen to in the kitchen. I sprinkled in my favorite opera arias and then topped the list off with some Coltrane and Bill Evans.

When I was done, I was struck by how the playlist really told a story of who I was. It captured so many different periods in my life and, in doing so, all sorts of feelings and emotions rose to the surface. It was powerful stuff, and I was blown away by how the music was able to transcend both time and space, taking me back to special moments along my journey. (That made me realize I also needed to add some Journey.)

As I sat listening, I saw how playlists were really a lot like fingerprints. Each person's list is different and unique.

And the power of music isn't just limited to memories. Music can also help motivate, excite, and inspire us now. It can help us cross the finish line of a marathon, write a novel, keep us going on that long lonely road trip.

Music is beautiful.

Today's Assignment:

1. Set your morning intention.
2. See the beauty in your day and record it later in your journal.

Extra Credit: *See the Beauty* Playlist

Professional athletes know the power of music. It's no coincidence that they're wearing those headphones as they jump off the team bus before a game, listening to music that will inspire them.

So why not you? Why not put together a playlist to enhance your own success in the *See the Beauty* program and in your life in general?

Put together a group of songs that evoke powerful emotions of happiness, joy, and excitement. Spend some time doing this. Start with a few favorites, but then add in some new songs.

Listen to your playlist daily, as you're getting ready in the morning, in the car on the way to work, when you're cooking dinner. Update the list often, adding and deleting songs to keep it fresh.

Extra, Extra Credit: Your Life in Music

Make a playlist of some of those meaningful tunes from your past. Write in your journal about the songs, why they are important, and what kinds of memories you associate with them.

DAY 26: HATING ON PARADISE

Trade your expectation for appreciation and the world changes instantly.

Tony Robbins

When I arrived in paradise, I really hated it.

I waited in the outdoor baggage claim area swimming in a river of sweat while my husband and daughter searched for our luggage at the far end of the carousel. I couldn't breathe. Couldn't think. The thick, humid air clung to my body like plastic wrap, smothering any good cheer about being off the plane after a long flight. And while my fellow passengers happily stripped down into shorts and tees, I was held prisoner in my all-in-one sweater-shirt that seemed like a good idea back in rainy Portland. There was nothing to do but drip and drip some more.

I stared at the palm trees painted to the sky.

"Where are the trade winds?" I said as we headed to the car rental lot. "It's supposed to be breezy in Hawaii, right?"

"Take it easy," Joe said. "We just got here."

But the heat and stillness in Maui continued. And it wasn't just the lack of wind that made me whine. The humidity level soared while a high surf warning was issued, which meant that all the beaches were closed to swimming and snorkeling. And because nobody could safely jump into the ocean for relief, the pool at our hotel turned into a sardine container packed with blotchy tourists splashing around in the bright aqua water.

Joe suggested that we go ahead and rent the snorkel equipment anyway, even though the weather forecast called for the high surf to stick around for our entire trip. I argued, but went along with the idea in the end. We got our masks and fins and breathing tubes and locked them in the trunk and then turned our attention to other activities, like taking pictures and driving up and down the coast and visiting shopping centers. We made plans to go to Haleakalā National Park, but my heart wasn't in it. All I really wanted to do was snorkel through schools of Moorish Idols and Ornate Wrasses and Angelfish, swim with Humu Humu Nuku Nuku Apua'a and giant green sea turtles. Maybe even see a barracuda or two at Black Rock.

As the days passed everything seemed to just get worse.

Our room was loud and hot. We spent boatloads of money on average lunches and dinners. We passed hordes of grumpy zombies lumbering down the walking path that hugged the coast. As we drove around the island searching for other things to do, a guy in a van narrowly missed smashing into our Cruiser before throwing a "hang loose" sign out the window.

"Paradise lost," I whispered, shaking my head.

It all got me wondering if we had been sucked into the public relations scam of the century. If the island was really nothing more than a swampy tourist trap overflowing with bad food and watered-down drinks.

On the next day relief finally came, but in a totally different way from what I was expecting.

And it all started with a tree.

I had never seen a banyan tree and the giant one in downtown Lahaina more than captured my attention with its massive root system and sweeping branches that stretched out over an entire city block. It stood 60 feet high and took up two-thirds of an acre with dangling vines and 12 major trunks. Planted in 1873, it was the largest banyan tree in the state.

It was also incredible.

There was something about standing next to such magnificence that helped put me back on track.

After all, I reminded myself, I was in Maui! It had been a dream for decades to visit this tropical island, and here I finally was, surrounded by a vast, wild, and dazzling ocean.

So instead of complaining about the heat and wishing I was doing something else, I began to accept everything exactly as it was, sweat and all. And within minutes I started seeing beauty all around me. Not the underwater world I was expecting to see when I was reading guidebooks back on the mainland, but a beautiful world nonetheless that had escaped my sight even though I had been standing right in the middle of it.

We walked around town and this time I really paid attention to the blue Hawaiian sky and the red hibiscus flowers that seemed to be everywhere. I inhaled the sweet fruit-scented air and listened to the infectious ukulele music streaming out from the stores we passed.

There was the beauty in my daughter's grin when she bought a turtle wind chime secretly for my husband, and beauty in her laughter when I showed her all the plastic "Bruddah" hula dancers up on a shelf. There were wooden tiki gods and little flower earrings and there was Joe, all serious as he looked through a rack of vintage Hawaiian shirts.

And at the end of the afternoon, there was even a rather delicious pulled pork sandwich at a little cafe.

When we got back to the hotel we passed by those same tourists crowded in the pool, but now I noticed that they were laughing (and red as beets). We took a little break upstairs and drank pineapple-infused rum and analyzed the plot of an old *Hawaii Five-O* episode that we had seen the night before. As the day faded, we walked over to the beach to see the sunset. It was postcard-perfect, an array of pinks and oranges and purples spread out across a massive sky, and we watched for a long time, quiet as shadows with our toes in the sand and the surf in our ears.

Standing there in the twilight, I knew that I had learned something important.

When I had been focusing on the "should be's," I made myself miserable and missed a lot of beauty. But when I shifted my attention and accepted things as they were, I saw beauty everywhere. I had finally learned to breathe easy in the sticky, tropical paradise, and nothing had changed except me. It was an inside job all the way.

It was a good lesson, something I would bring back with me.

Later that evening, as I slept, I thought I heard the sound of palm fronds moving and sure enough in the morning there was a sweet breeze blowing in from the northeast. By midday, the high surf miraculously settled down and all the beaches were opened. And although I was thrilled to unlock the car trunk and start exploring that new world under the sea, I wasn't desperate about it anymore. I knew that no matter what, I'd be able to see any kind of beauty that came my way.

Today's Assignment:

1. Set your morning intention.
2. Find at least 10 points of beauty in your day and record them in your journal later. (Remember that you don't have to draw all ten, but make a list.)

Extra Credit: Beauty Missed

Take a few moments and think back to a time when something similar happened to you, when you didn't see the beauty because you were holding certain expectations. Write about your experience in your journal, answering some or all of the following questions:

- What was the event and what were the expectations you had going in?
- Did you have a transformation where you were able to let go of those expectations and just see the beauty in what was around you?
- What was your process for seeing the beauty in that one event? For me, it was a little bit of time and seeing that banyan tree. What did you need to shift from disappointment to appreciation? Time? Someone else pointing it out? Alcohol?

• Is there something that troubles you now where you could apply this same process and alter your perception? Can you find beauty in a frustrating situation?

DAY 27: STROLL AMONG THE SAGUAROS

The truth is, we know so little about life, we don't really know what the good news is and what the bad news is.

Kurt Vonnegut

As I was walking along a stretch of Saguaro National Park one morning it came to me that my short hike was a perfect example of what the *See the Beauty* program is all about.

There were some challenging things along the trail, things you have to watch out for. Like nearly all the flora is covered in sharp needles or prickly thorns. And the blazing sun can take you down faster than an Old West gunslinger. And there are dangerous creatures lurking about, like the six types of venomous snakes and the killer bees, the grunting javelinas and stealth mountain lions, the scorpions and poisonous spiders and Gila monsters so tenacious that if you get bitten by one you'll have to bring it with you to the ER so doctors can cut it from your flesh.

Needless to say, as I walked alone my senses were heightened, the occasional noise in the brush causing a swarm of panic.

But after the first mile or so, when I relaxed a little, I was able to really see it.

Beauty was everywhere.

Jagged and moody mountains rose in the distance, white flowers bloomed on the tips of the saguaros, a quail family scurried behind the prickly pear. A huge jackrabbit darted across the path, birds sang, hawks soared in the clear sky, a soft breeze blew into my face.

Sure, there were frightening aspects to the journey, but there was also tremendous beauty. And really, when I was able to push aside the fear, when I was able to focus on the good and let go of the other things, what was left was an incredible wonderland.

Just like in life.

Today's Assignment:

1. Set your morning intention.
2. See the beauty in your day and capture those moments in your journal.

Extra Credit: Heart Therapy

I love the heart as a symbol. Whenever I see one, it reminds me of who I want to be in the world—kind, loving, peaceful, open, and non-judgmental. Sometimes though it feels like I'm very far away from that person, especially when I'm feeling scared or angry.

So not too long ago I started drawing hearts. Charcoal is great for this particular art project because you can play with it on the paper, really getting into it. And because it's a simple shape drawn over and over and over again, it's a perfect activity to combine with meditation or mindfulness or prayer.

Spend about 10 minutes or so for every heart. Sometimes, if I know of someone who is having a hard time, I'll think about them while I draw. Kind of like a heart prayer. Or I'll let my mind focus on opening my own heart, to be kinder and gentler.

So get some charcoal and some thick paper and sketch some hearts.

DAY 28: BEARING WITNESS TO BEAUTY

Have compassion for everyone you meet... You do not know what wars are going on down there where the spirit meets the bone.

Miller Williams

Whether it's noticing the beauty of a rainbow, or being involved in the beauty of trying to stop an injustice, beauty is everywhere. It's in participating in a protest march, it's in a cascading waterfall, it's in helping an addicted brother get off prescription pain pills. It's in trying to make things better for others and trying to make things better for you.

Seeing the beauty is about acknowledging all the blessings that surround you.

It's about noticing the light in the world. It's about spending just a small amount of time each day bearing witness to the beauty in your life.

Today's Assignment:

1. Set the morning intention.
2. See the beauty in your day and record it later in your journal.

Extra Credit: Do Something Nice

Do something nice for someone today.

DAY 29: THE BEAUTY OF POETRY

There are no happy endings.
Endings are the saddest part,
So just give me a happy middle
And a very happy start.

Shel Silverstein

My best friend Ann and I did all sorts of fun things together when we were in the sixth grade. And even though we lived in completely different worlds (she was from the top of the hill and I was from the "wrong" side of Ventura Boulevard), we found common ground in Mr. Milan's class at Sherman Oaks Elementary.

We spent our days reading, learning new math, and writing reports. We ate frozen blueberries in the mornings, sneaking handfuls out of our lunches until our purple fingers gave us away. At recess we flew through the air like plastic monkeys off the rings and twirled like acrobats on the bars. We played hopscotch under a smelly cloud of eucalyptus while we talked about TV shows and spent hours practicing the Hustle for graduation.

It was a very special year, a year when we ruled life, or at least thought we did until we learned the truth a little later in junior high school.

It was also the year when we both fell in love with Shel Silverstein.

We'd found his book, *Where the Sidewalk Ends*, and immediately began gobbling down the poems in huge quantities like candy on Halloween night. We passed the book back and forth between our desks, giggling and smiling and pointing to our favorites, like the one about little Peggy Ann McKay or Lazy Jane or Hector the Collector. And that one with the crazy boy who loved putting Band-Aids all over his body, and that other one with the kid who put a toilet plunger on their head because "Teddy said it was a hat."

There was a poem about a guy turning into a TV because he watched too much of it, and another about a boy being eaten by a boa constrictor. And of course that one about the girl who refused to take the garbage out and another about a kid who really wasn't that smart even though he thought he was.

The poems were about things we could relate to. Pretending to be sick when we didn't want to go to school, dropping an ice cream cone on the ground, getting tangled in a jump rope. Wanting to fly. The book was brilliant and poignant and silly all at the same time. And we loved it.

"Come in, come in!" Shel shouted in the first pages. Everyone was invited to the poetry party: dreamers, hopers, wishers, and liars. He wanted us all.

Ann and I loved that book so much that we decided that we needed to take the poems "to the street." It was poetry that demanded to be shared, words that needed to be heard, the kind that we knew could stop a four-square game in its tracks. So during recess we started walking around the playground with *Where the Sidewalk Ends* in our hands and read out loud to anybody who would listen. Kids, yard teachers, visitors. Everybody. And not to our surprise, they did stop and listen! Balls were tucked under arms and for a few moments a quiet settled in around us and smiles swept across faces as we read.

Shel Silverstein stayed with me my entire life, each new release finding a place on my bookshelf and following me through high school and college, motherhood and beyond. I read his poems to my children, again and again and again until they grew into adults. When I became an elementary school teacher, I read the poems to my students and then had them make posters of their favorite ones to put up around the school so even more kids could read them and laugh out loud.

I've been thinking a lot about Shel lately, probably because I recently visited Key West for a writers' conference and drove by the house where he used to live.

When I saw the house, I didn't have the joyful reaction I was expecting. Instead, my chest tightened and a thick sorrow settled inside when our tour guide informed us that this was the place where Shel had died of a heart attack nearly 20 years ago. This was where Shel's sidewalk ended, I remembered thinking as I blinked away a tear. This was where his poetry died.

But as I caught a glimpse of the sparkling ocean a moment later, I realized that I wasn't seeing it right at all.

Because the real Shel will never die. Not with all the love he sowed with his words. Not as long as his poems are available in classrooms and bookstores, on the Internet and in libraries.

It all made me think how very beautiful it was that Shel Silverstein shared his poetry with us, leaving his magic here. And about how even decades after his death he continues to make the world a better, softer place.

[Note: Shortly after my visit to Key West, Hurricane Irma destroyed Shel's house.]

Today's Assignment:

1. Set the morning intention.
2. See the beauty in your day and record it later in your journal.

Extra Credit: A Childhood Memory Haiku

For today's extra credit, write a haiku about something special you remember from your childhood.

Haiku is a type of Japanese poetry that reflects on nature and feelings. There are usually three lines with five syllables in the first line, seven syllables in the second, and five syllables in the third. Copy your poem in your journal and add an illustration.

Example:

Shel Silverstein rules
He wrote Where the Sidewalk Ends
His poetry lives!

DAY 30: THE BEAUTY IN YOUR NEW STORY

Dwell on the beauty of life. Watch the stars, and see yourself running with them.

Marcus Aurelius

I am a storyteller. I make my living creating characters, imagining scenes, developing plots, and finding that elusive balance between keeping readers interested and not telling them too much too soon. To do this, I use the power of focus. Much like a camera lens, I zero in on the elements of the story that I want to divulge, keeping everything else fuzzy in the background.

I might have my main character talking to a woman in front of the library. If I don't want readers to know just yet that the woman is a ghost, I won't write about the people on the street walking by throwing shade at someone apparently talking to herself. And I also won't mention that the woman is translucent, her eyes opaque. Using this kind of selective focus gives me the ability to tell the story that I want to tell.

When you think about it, we are all storytellers in our own lives. Depending on our storytelling, our lives are good or bad, pleasing or frustrating, fun or boring, full of beauty or full of a hundred shades of gray. We focus on certain things while obscuring others, pushing them into the background.

Most of the scenes that we do choose to focus on will support whatever narrative we believe about our lives. For example, if your narrative goes something like "I'm a lucky person," the camera will pan over your day, zooming in tight on that parking space you found earlier, getting that very last four-cheese bagel at the lunch cart, and that pillow fight you had with your kids. But if your narrative is more like "I can't win," then the camera will focus on different things, like the maxed out credit cards, the long commute, and the sister who calls five times a day needing things.

Your *See the Beauty* journal is the story of who you are when you take the time to focus on all the beauty in your life. It's a new story about the old you, a fresh (or *re*freshed) way of looking at what your life is really about: adventure, new experiences, fun, love, excitement, and beauty.

Sure, in every life there will be challenges and hard times, but those times are only part of the story. It's not the entire story no matter how much it tries to be. The story you want to get into the habit of telling is right there in the pages of your *See the Beauty* journal.

Now it's time to go back and read this new, powerful narrative, filled with plenty of examples and illustrations that support the story that, yes, you really do have a most magnificent life filled with so, so much beauty.

Today's Assignment:

1. Set your morning intention.
2. See the beauty in your day and record it in your journal.
3. Read over your *See the Beauty* journal from start to finish, acknowledging your new story.

Extra Credit: Looking Back, Part 1

If you wrote a letter to yourself as part of the first extra credit assignment, now is the time to go back and read it. Has anything changed in how you look at your life?

Extra, Extra Credit: Looking Back, Part 2

After spending time looking over your journal, write about the experience, making sure to address the following points:
- Write a few sentences about the story of your life chronicled in your *See the Beauty* journal.
- After you finished looking over the month, how did it leave you feeling?
- What types of beauty did you tend to notice throughout the month? List some of the recurring themes you encountered. (Snow? Swimming? Your soulmate? Starbucks coffee? Cooking dinner in your remodeled kitchen?)
- Can you see the new story of you, how you are an amazing person on this amazing journey called life?
- Write a little about all the beauty you regularly see now in your life.
- What is your plan for continuing along the *See the Beauty* path? How can you see even more beauty in the coming months?

Whenever I take the time to look back, I always feel that the exercise adds another layer of beauty to my life and always leaves me feeling full of gratitude. I find myself smiling, whispering things like, "Oh, yeah, I forgot about that chile apple pie with pine nuts that was so delicious" or "Oh, yeah, I forgot about how we all sat around and drank beer and played the Oregon Trail card game while it snowed outside." Those memories and good associations flood back, leaving me feeling very blessed all over again.

And if you're like me, you'll be pulling out your journal(s) many times in the coming years, reliving those great memories. It's like those beautiful moments keep exploding into more and more moments, like fireworks in a big night sky that's suddenly not so dark but filled with light and promise.

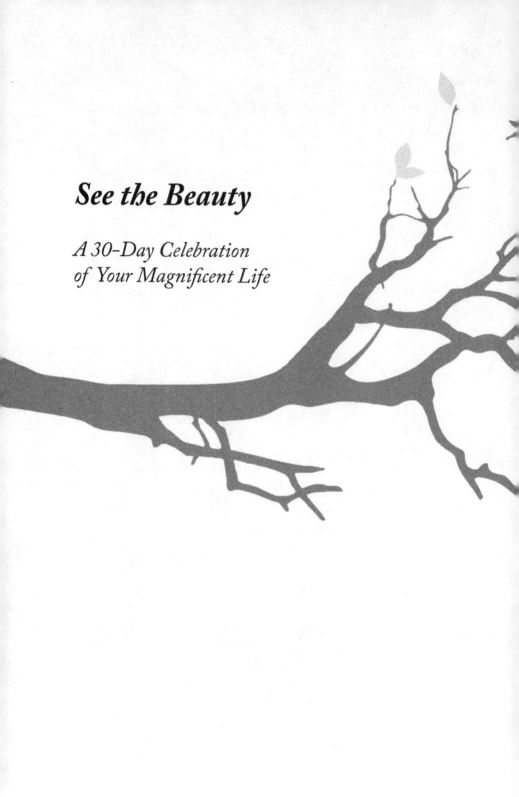

See the Beauty

*A 30-Day Celebration
of Your Magnificent Life*

MOVING FORWARD

I AM YOU

We teach best what we most need to learn.

Richard Bach

I've learned over the years that starting a new habit in life isn't about suddenly finding yourself at the top of the mountain. It's about taking small steps every day, consistently inching up the trail, and enjoying the journey.

A case in point is a walk I took the other day while negative thoughts took me for a ride. Again. I did this even after having filled countless *See the Beauty* journals and believing in the program with my heart and soul. I did this even though I knew better.

But after I had thought about it, I realized that falling into that old familiar pattern of negative thinking served as a great reminder that change is never easy, never complete, how it's about moving ahead and sometimes falling back. And it's about never giving up.

What I'm trying to say is that I'm only a little bit farther up the trail from where you are now, lighting small fires along the way, gently calling out to remind you that your life is amazing and wonderful just as it is right now. We are pilgrims on this journey called life, surrounded in beauty.

WAYS TO KEEP SEEING THE BEAUTY

Okay, so you've put in your 30 days and you're happy with the results. You're feeling great and seeing more beauty than ever before. You've even made a vow to continue journaling all the beauty in your life forever.

But as we all know, even the best of intentions can get derailed. So here are a few ideas to help you maintain your new habit:

1. Visit the *See the Beauty* website at SeetheBeautyProject.com and read the latest blogs and learn about upcoming live workshops with Jools.
2. Take an online *See the Beauty* class—it's a great way to continue the practice. Go to SeetheBeautyProject.com, enter the code EBOOK50 at checkout, and save 50%.
3. Follow *See the Beauty* on Instagram @SeetheBeautyProject for daily inspiration.
4. Start your own *See the Beauty* group with your family and friends and meet once a week.
5. Join the *See the Beauty* community on Facebook and chat and share with other people who are also making an effort to see the beauty in their lives.
6. Make colorful little notes and leave them around your house, office, and car to remind you to look for beauty.
7. Treat yourself to some really nice art supplies every so often.
8. Continue to make inspirational playlists and listen to them.
9. Create your own YouTube channel and collect some inspirational videos like Brother David Steindl-Rast's *A Good Day*.
10. Catch up on all the extra credit assignments.

FREQUENTLY ASKED QUESTIONS

Sometimes I get questions like...

I don't have time to read all the essays in the book. Can I skip the reading and just do my journaling?

Yes! Doing the daily entries in your *See the Beauty* journal is the most important part of this program. The essays are only there to help you keep the journal and encourage you. You can read them at your convenience, or not at all. The journal is the key.

Can't I just take pictures of the beautiful things during my day instead of having to write and draw in a journal?

Of course you should take photos of all the wonder you notice throughout your day. It's a great way of seeing the beauty and will add depth to the program. But don't replace the journaling with photography. Doing a daily entry as instructed will take you to a deeper level of appreciation. Yes, we live in amazing times, and yes taking photos is fun. But remember that *See the Beauty* is also about cultivating a meditative habit of reflection and appreciation that is best achieved unplugged and through journaling. By adding the art component to your practice, it helps to slow down your mind so you can dive deeper into the experience.

Well, okay, but then is it possible to do an online journal? I promise I'll reflect as I'm putting my techie art together.

The bottom line is you can do it however you like. And seeing the beauty in your own way is always a good idea. But again,

I would recommend doing the program as it is written here, with your journal and pencils.

Jools, so much of this book seems to be about you. What about me? Where do I fit in?
You're right and there's no point denying it. To a great degree, this book *is* about me. But by completing this program something interesting will happen. By the end of the 30 days, you will have your own book. A book about *you.*

I've skimmed through the book and noticed there is an assignment every day and also extra credit every day. I can't do it all! I don't have time to do the extra credit. Is that okay?
Of course.
The extra credit is there for those who have the time and desire to do a little more. And while I've included an extra credit each day, I realize that most people won't always have the time. Also, there might be some that you are not interested in. They're just ideas to enhance the program.

What if I really want to use three or four journal pages a day because I like art more than words. Is that okay?
Yes!

I've had a day from Hell. I can't see any beauty and the last thing I want to do after getting a bad review at work is to open my See the Beauty *journal. What should I do?*
Be easy about all of this. This is your practice. First, acknowledge that you had a bad day at work. Close your eyes and take a few deep breaths. Then do something silly, even though you don't feel like it. Tickle yourself or jump up and down while repeating, "I am not my job." Then spend just two or three minutes looking beyond your challenging day and write a few phrases about some of the beauty that was on the fringes, waiting for you to see it. Or, just take the day off if you have to and steer yourself gently back to your journal tomorrow.

How am I supposed to see any beauty when there's so much chaos in the world?

There has always been chaos since the beginning of time, just like there's always been beauty. The two exist side by side, and the choice is yours in terms of which you want to focus on.

I did the 30-day program and have tried to continue, but I need a break. Is it okay to take a break?

Of course. People do *See the Beauty* in different ways. You can continuously keep a journal or you can do it in 30-day chunks three to four times a year. Do whatever works for you.

Help! I can't stop seeing the beauty even though I've tried. Damn it, Jools. What have you done?

Sorry.

I like your ideas here, I really do. But I gotta ask. How do you explain all the evil in the world?

I can't.

I don't know why there is a meanness in the world, why hate and evil exist. And while I'm sure that some people who do terrible things would claim to see beauty in their actions, we know this is false because there is never beauty in hurting others. Not ever.

But I do have a very strong understanding of the beauty in love. And not just loving others, but in loving yourself, your life, your day.

Love eclipses everything dark, everything bad. Love is the answer. And when we realize this, then nothing dark or evil wins.

EXTRA CREDIT

All the extra credit assignments in one convenient place...

Day 1: **Extra Credit:** Write a Letter to Yourself

Write a letter to yourself, answering the following questions:

- How much appreciation and gratitude do you feel on a daily basis?
- Why are you doing this program?
- What are some negative beliefs you have regarding your life right now?
- What are you hoping to achieve by the end of this 30-day program?

Write this letter on a separate piece of paper that can be tucked away in the back pocket in your journal (or taped if there is no pocket). On Day 30 you'll return to the letter and read it.

Day 2: **Extra Credit:** New Job Exercise

This exercise will expand the way you think about color. Pretend that you've just been hired at the Sherman Gilliams Paint Company. Your job is to come up with whimsical new names for the colors below. For example, instead of just red, it's *Roses at Twilight Red*, instead of plain green, it's *Van Gogh Green*.

Be creative and have fun! Name paint colors however you wish, after favorite times of the day, favorite characters from a book, a scene out of a movie (*Casablanca Mauve, Elizabeth Bennet Blue, Out of the Past Gray*). Record the new names you've created along with swatches of color in your journal.

Here is the list of colors you've been assigned: red, yellow, green, blue, purple, pink, brown, black, white, and orange. Feel free to add more of your own if you find yourself inspired.

Day 3: **Extra Credit:** Make a List of 10 Things You Love Doing

In your journal make a list of 10 things you love doing. Be specific. For example, if you enjoy going on long bike rides, write about where you love to go. If you like staying up late watching movies, note what kinds of movies you watch. If pub crawls are your thing, write about your favorite ales (if you can remember). Add some color and/or illustrations.

Day 4: **Extra Credit:** Heart of the Matter

Supplies needed: A large sheet of blank paper, colored pencils, pens, or crayons.

This exercise is a nice way of getting a visual portrait of who you are and what's important to you. You'll be making a heart that will represent you and all the things that you love.

- First, make a list of the things that matter most to you, the things closest to your heart. (For example, family and friends, cooking risotto, Italian opera, skiing, kayaking, writing novels, walking and hiking, snow, sunshine, birds, pine trees, colorful autumn leaves, snorkeling, chocolate chip cookies, road trips.)
- Next, draw a large heart on a large piece of paper.
- Transfer the items from your list onto different parts of the heart, leaving room for small illustrations.
- Add background color(s).

This activity takes a while, so don't feel compelled to finish it in one sitting. But when you're done, take a look at it. Is it a good representation of who you are? Would it tell "your story" if a stranger looked at it?

Day 5: **Extra Credit:** Write a "Beauty is..." Poem

Write your own free verse poem about beauty. Use the words, "Beauty is..." to start each line and complete the sentences with specific examples from your own life.

Write at least 10 lines.

Because it's a "free verse" poem, you don't have to worry about rhyming or any other formal pattern. Just let the words flow.

Do a first draft on a separate piece of paper, and then copy the final version into your *See the Beauty* journal.

Day 6: **Extra Credit:** *Suiseki*

Go outside today and try some *Suiseki*, the ancient Japanese art of stone appreciation. You're looking for rocks that suggest natural scenes, animals, or figures. It's kind of like that game you played as a kid, lying in the grass, looking for shapes up in the clouds. It's basically the same concept in *Suiseki*, except you'll be looking down at rocks and stones.

For this practice, rocks should never be modified. When you find one (or two), bring it home, draw a picture of it in your *See the Beauty* journal, and display the rock in a special place.

Day 7: **Extra Credit:** Georgia O'Keeffe Pastel Drawing

In this extra credit assignment, you are going to draw a flower, focusing on the details.

- First, you'll need a large piece of paper (I like to square it off for this activity), a pencil, pastels (if you don't have pastels, use colored pencils or watercolor pencils), and a flower.
- Give yourself plenty of time to study the flower.

- Using a pencil, sketch exactly what you see, drawing the intricate details. Draw it big like Georgia O'Keeffe. (You might even want to look up some of her work on the Internet if you're not familiar with her.)
- Have a goal of making your flower touch all four sides of the paper.
- Don't leave the background white. I usually draw a blue sky peeking out from behind my giant flower.

Day 8: **Extra Credit:** Dance, Dance, Dance

For today's extra credit choreograph an interpretive dance representing your day. Add music if you think it will help. Good luck.

Day 9: **Extra Credit:** Day and Night

Set aside time today to visit a place—any place of your choosing as long as it's safe. Visit sometime during the day and then again at night. What differences do you notice? How does it look? Does the air smell different? Is it crowded or quiet? Does the mood feel different? Which visit did you like better? Why? Write about it in your journal.

Day 10: **Extra Credit:** Those Smaller Moments

Think back on a time when you had one of those big moments of beauty. It could be anything as long as it was big for you. Write a few lines about the beauty of that event, and then go a little bit deeper, and write some more about those smaller moments of beauty that were surrounding it. Give yourself enough time to think through this exercise, listing as many moments as possible.

Day 11: **Extra Credit:** 10 Points

In your journal list 10 *points* of beauty from each of your five senses that you've experienced recently.

Day 12: **Extra Credit:** Habits

Think about some of the daily habits you have in your life right now. Write about them in your *See the Beauty* journal, addressing the following:
  • List all the activities that you have gotten into the habit of doing every single day (brushing your teeth, exercising, eating kale).
  • How were you successful in creating a daily routine for those activities? What motivates you to continue?
  • Are there some habits that you've stopped? Why did you stop doing them? How can you apply the success of your daily habits to the *See the Beauty* program?

Day 13: **Extra Credit:** Be a Poet

Be a poet in your life today no matter where you go. Notice everything. Take a few extra minutes noticing the things you usually ignore. Expand your world, soak it all in.

Day 14: **Extra Credit:** Thinking Back

Think back to a particularly hard period in your life. Write a little bit about it in your journal, making sure to answer the following questions:

  • Now that you've had some time to reflect, were there any moments of beauty that you might not have noticed during that tough time?
  • Did you learn anything after going through that particular challenging event?
  • Did you learn something that you can use in the future?

Day 15: **Extra Credit:** Crossing Over

Have you had any experience or interaction with the creative process? If so, write or draw about it in your journal.

If not, would you like to? To unlock the magic, all you hav to do is choose something that you like doing (painting, writing, drawing, sculpting, knitting, singing, running, dancing) and start spending a lot of time doing it. Commit to going to a deeper level and you'll find your muse.

Day 16: **Extra Credit:** Right Now

From where you are, look around you and notice the beauty. Don't write it or illustrate it, just spend a few moments right now appreciating it.

Day 17: **Extra Credit:** Pets!

Have you experienced the beauty of the animal kingdom? If so, spend some time writing about a favorite memory or two of a pet or an animal you've observed (your cat kneading the blanket at your feet, a crow hopping around, a coyote strolling down a suburban street at dusk like he owned it). When you're done add in some illustrations and color.

Day 18: **Extra Credit:** Dreams

Do a little dream analysis on yourself, answering the following questions:

- What dreams did you have when you were young?
- What dreams have you been able to turn into reality?
- What were some of the strategies you used for turning a dream into reality?
- What dreams do you have now?
- What are some strategies you could use to make them come true?

Day 19: **Extra Credit:** Saying No

For many people, women especially, saying no is a hard thing to do. Along with our innate sense of compassion and caring, many of us have also been raised to be people pleasers,

...ifficult when it comes to putting our own needs

...ying no to the things you don't want to do is really
...ng care of yourself. And I can attest that it is never too
that, never too late to learn.

...So for today, write a little bit about saying no in your jour-
..., making sure to express your thoughts and feelings on the
...dea of you rejecting something as well as answering the following questions:

- How does saying no make you feel? Guilty? Happy? Full of angst? Scared?
- When was the last time you said no to something that you didn't want to do? When was the last time you said yes to something you didn't want to do?
- How does not saying no (i.e., saying, "Yes, sure, whatever you need") make you feel when you really don't want to do something?
- Do you think that learning how to say no would be beneficial? If so, how would learning that new skill change your life? What would you do less of and what would you have more time for?

Day 20: **Extra Credit:** Mindful Eating

Be present during an entire meal. The next meal you sit down to eat, make an effort to be as present as possible. Even if there are other people around, make it a point to focus on what you're eating. What does the food taste like? Can you detect subtle flavors that you didn't before? Try to clear your mind and focus your entire attention on every aspect of the meal. Chew slowly, savoring every bite. When your mind starts to wander, gently direct it back to the present moment.

Day 21: **Extra Credit:** I Am Poem

Writing poetry can be fun and working on this "I Am" poem can also be a great learning experience. Choose from the lines below to complete your poem. You don't have to use all of them. Fill in personal details as you go and be creative with your answers, thinking outside the box.

Copy the finished product into your *See the Beauty* journal. Add some color and a few illustrations. Celebrate the beautiful you!

"I Am" Poem

I am… (your name)
I love… (list at least one thing)
I know… (list at least one thing)
I believe… (list at least one thing)
I wish… (list at least one thing)
I want… (list at least one thing)
I'm excited when… (list at least one thing)
I'm happiest when… (list at least one thing)
I dream about… (list at least one thing)
I love learning about… (list at least one thing)
I love going to…. (list at least one thing)
I love creating… (list at least one thing)
I love hearing… (list at least one thing)
I love seeing… (list at least one thing)
I love feeling… (list at least one thing)
I love touching… (list at least one thing)
I love smelling… (list at least one thing)
I am… (name)

Example:

Jools
I love long road trips through the desert, first snows, sparkling swimming pools, novels about stolen art and WWII, ocean waves pounding the shore, sitting by a bonfire, hanging out with family and friends.
I know how to paddle on the Green River, how to write a book, the storylines of five operas, how to make gnocchi while surrounded in clouds of flour dust.
I believe in the magic of the Universe.
I wish for inner peace, more trips back home to Bend, a Pad Thai

recipe that knocks my socks off, to sit in restaurants overlooking the Amalfi Coast.
I'm excited when the Dodgers win, when the World Cup begins, for Sunday night dinners, packing for a trip and also returning home. I'm happiest when writing, eating good food, drinking good wine, hiking in red rock country, cooking, when my toes are in the sand. I dream about tropical islands, Florence, hitting number one on the NYT Bestseller list.
Jools

Day 22: **Extra Credit:** Beauty in the Bad

Have you ever had an experience like the one described above? A bad job, a horrible relationship, a tough childhood. While all of these things are hardships, there are often gems beneath the surface of the experience if you take a little time to look.

Pick something that was hard for you and think about it for a while. When you're ready, write a paragraph or two describing the bad points in your journal. Then, write about the lessons you learned, and/or the beauty you found in that situation, making sure to answer the following questions:

- Did you eventually find some good in the bad?
- Was there any other beauty surrounding that event?
- Can you see that this might be a good story to reflect on from time to time, reminding yourself that there can be beauty in the difficult situations you now face?

Extra, Extra Credit: Get Artsy

Creating art is a great way to de-stress after a bad day at work, letting your worries evaporate for a little while. So today spend some time creating art. It can be any kind of art that makes you happy, from crocheting to painting to sewing to drawing. Here are a few "artsy" ideas that I love doing when I have a little time.

• *Charcoal Sketching...* Of all the art mediums, I find this one to be the most relaxing.
• *Alcohol Inks...* Alcohol inks can be found at most art and craft stores, as well as online. If you're not familiar with them, look up some examples on YouTube to see what they are about. They are very abstract and colorful and it's the kind of art that always turns out great no matter what you do.
• *Paper Marbling...* Paper marbling is one of my all-time favorite activities, although to do it the "old-fashioned" way, it takes a lot of time, preparation, and skill. But recently, I came across a product that makes it super simple. It's called *Easy Marble.*

Day 23: **Extra Credit:** 100 Points of Beauty

This is one of my favorite exercises. You will need some time to complete it, so if you're busy today, schedule this for later.

Make a list of 100 points of beauty that have happened in your life (so far). The list should include the big things, like getting your college degree or going to Paris or bringing home your new puppy, and little things, like smelling orange blossoms in the air for the first time on a spring evening in Tucson. Don't think too hard on one particular thing, just keep your pencil moving.

Make sure to number the list as you go and use just a few words or phrases for each item (no complete sentences necessary).

Two tips for success in this exercise:

• Before you start, make a thoughtful list of 10 important things you feel you *must* include, such as giving birth to your children or marrying your high school sweetheart. Include everything that might leave you feeling awful if you accidently left it off your *100 Points of Beauty* list. (Because, believe it or not, it's easy to do as you get going in this stream-of-consciousness exercise). So take the first few minutes at the beginning and include those large things so you can let your mind run wild on everything else.

- The second tip for this exercise is to make it fun! Put on some music and let your mind wander back into those great moments of beauty that you've had in your life. Add a glass of wine or sparkling soda, a lit candle. This is, after all, a celebration of your life.

Day 24: **Extra Credit:** Reflecting

Write a few paragraphs about your own learning experiences, making sure to touch on the following:

- List some of your favorite subjects in school. What did you love learning? Are you still interested in them and have you continued learning?
- Have you taken any classes recently that you love (painting, knitting, hip hop dancing, paddle boarding, web design, *See the Beauty*)?
- List the different things that you've learned this year. (Did you learn more about the game of baseball? Chiaroscuro? How to make a port and fig sauce?)
- Make of list of some of the things you would like to learn about in the coming year.

Day 25: **Extra Credit:** *See the Beauty* Playlist

Professional athletes know the power of music. It's no coincidence that they're wearing those headphones as they jump off the team bus before a game, listening to music that will inspire them.

So why not you? Why not put together a playlist to enhance your own success in the *See the Beauty* program and in your life in general?

Put together a group of songs that evoke powerful emotions of happiness, joy, and excitement. Spend some time doing this. Start with a few favorites, but then add in some new songs.

Listen to your playlist daily, as you're getting ready in the morning, in the car on the way to work, when you're cooking dinner. Update the list often, adding and deleting songs to keep it fresh.

Extra, Extra Credit: Your Life in Music

Make a playlist of some of those meaningful tunes from your past. Write in your journal about the songs, why they are important, and what kinds of memories you associate with them.

Day 26: **Extra Credit:** Beauty Missed

Take a few moments and think back to a time when something similar happened to you, when you didn't see the beauty because you were holding certain expectations. Write about your experience in your journal, answering some or all of the following questions:

• What was the event and what were the expectations you had going in?
• Did you have a transformation where you were able to let go of those expectations and just see the beauty in what was around you?
• What was your process for seeing the beauty in that one event? For me, it was a little bit of time and seeing that banyan tree. What did you need to shift from disappointment to appreciation? Time? Someone else pointing it out? Alcohol?
• Is there something that troubles you now where you could apply this same process and alter your perception? Can you find beauty in a frustrating situation?

Day 27: **Extra Credit:** Heart Therapy

I love the heart as a symbol. Whenever I see one, it reminds me of who I want to be in the world—kind, loving, peaceful, open, and non-judgmental. Sometimes though it feels like I'm very far away from that person, especially when I'm feeling scared or angry.

So not too long ago I started drawing hearts. Charcoal is great for this particular art project because you can play with it on the paper, really getting into it. And because it's a simple shape drawn over and over and over again, it's a perfect activity to combine with meditation or mindfulness or prayer.

Spend about 10 minutes or so for every heart. Sometimes, if I know of someone far away who is having a hard time, I'll think about them while I draw. Kind of like a heart prayer. Or I'll let my mind focus on opening my own heart, to be kinder and gentler.

So get some charcoal and some thick paper and sketch some hearts.

Day 28: **Extra Credit:** Do Something Nice

Do something nice for someone today.

Day 29: **Extra Credit:** A Childhood Memory Haiku

For today's extra credit, write a haiku about something special you remember from your childhood.

Haiku is a type of Japanese poetry that reflects on nature and feelings. There are usually three lines with five syllables in the first line, seven syllables in the second, and five syllables in the third. Copy your poem in your journal and add an illustration.

Example:

Shel Silverstein rules
He wrote Where the Sidewalk Ends
His poetry lives!

Day 30: **Extra Credit:** Looking Back, Part 1

If you wrote a letter to yourself as part of the first extra credit assignment, now is the time to go back and read it. Has anything changed in how you look at your life?

Extra, Extra Credit: Looking Back, Part 2

After spending time looking over your journal, write about the experience, making sure to address the following points:

- Write a few sentences about the story of your life chronicled in your *See the Beauty* journal.
- After you finished looking over the month, how did it leave you feeling?
- What types of beauty did you tend to notice throughout the month? List some of the recurring themes you encountered. (Snow? Swimming? Your soulmate? Starbucks coffee? Cooking dinner in your remodeled kitchen?)
- Can you see the new story of you, how you are an amazing person on this amazing journey called life?
- Write a little about all the beauty you regularly see now in your life.
- What is your plan for continuing along the *See the Beauty* path? How can you see even more beauty in the coming months?

Whenever I take the time to look back, I always feel that the exercise adds another layer of beauty to my life and always leaves me feeling full of gratitude. I find myself smiling, whispering things like, "Oh, yeah, I forgot about that chile apple pie with pine nuts that was so delicious" or "Oh, yeah, I forgot about how we all sat around and drank beer and played the Oregon Trail card game while it snowed outside." Those memories and good associations flood back, leaving me feeling very blessed all over again.

And if you're like me, you'll be pulling out your journal(s) many times in the coming years, reliving those great memories. It's like those beautiful moments keep exploding into more and more moments, like fireworks in a big night sky that's suddenly not so dark but filled with light and promise.

ACKNOWLEDGMENTS

May the sun bring you new energy by day
May the moon softly restore you by night
May the rain wash away your worries
May the breeze blow new strength into your being
May you walk gently through the world and know its beauty all the
days of your life.

Apache Blessing

I know I'm lucky.

I'm surrounded by so many beautiful people and I am immensely grateful to all who have helped create this book.

First, thank you to my incredibly cool, awesomely inspiring, always spirit-lifting and soul-raising family: Joe, Cassandra, Meg, and Jeff, Liti and Dewey, and the Ghost of Big Orange. I love you all so much and am appreciative that you are all in my life. Thank you for bringing happiness, laughter, and smarts into my world regularly and for helping me finish this book.

Thank you, Cassandra (aka Ms. Sawdust), for your huge heart, fierce attitude, for being an "Awesome A," and for adding so much light to my life *all* these years.

And, Meg, thank you for your sagacity, inspiration, and all the beauty you in bring into my world daily.

Thank you both for reminding me of that promise I made.

Jeff, thank you for your kindness, humor, and wit.

A huge hug to the original *See the Beauty* Facebook class and especially to those who stuck with it and completed the 30 days and then some: Donna, Sara, Tasha, Debbie, Jan, Molly, LJ, MM, Hilda, Susan, Anna, Lydia, Twila, Barbara, and Sheila. You are all so awesome. Thanks for helping to bring *See the Beauty* into the world.

Thank you and big hugs to Ann, who has been a part of my life for practically half a century now and made an appearance in the Shel Silverstein essay. While editing I had to cut out some fun parts from our sixth grade experience, but know that I will always remember pomegranates and going to that Bee Gees concert with your brother, Fashion Square on the weekends, and of course "this is a penny." It was one of those amazing years, and we really did rule the school for a little while. Yay, us!

And finally, a huge thank you to you, the reader, for finding this book. By seeing the beauty, you not only elevate your own life but contribute new light to the world.

I've spent the last seven years writing novels that focus on ghosts, criminal behavior, and evil. And now, here I am, telling people how to live their lives surrounded in beauty. It's kind of funny.

But it came to me recently that it's really all the same. That, in fact, I always write about the same thing: searching for light in the world, trying to find the good, and letting the darkness fall away.

By choosing to live in gratitude for our many blessings, we bear witness to the beauty in the world.

From the bottom of my heart, thank you all so much for being part of this *See the Beauty* journey.

Love,
Jools

OTHER BOOKS BY JOOLS SINCLAIR

The Forty-Four Series

Forty-Four
Forty-Four Book Two
Forty-Four Book Three
Forty-Four Book Four
Forty-Four Book Five
Forty-Four Book Six
Forty-Four Book Seven
Forty-Four Book Eight
Forty-Four Book Nine
Forty-Four Book Ten
Forty-Four Book Eleven
Forty-Four Book Twelve
Forty-Four Book Thirteen
Forty-Four Box Set Books 1-5
Forty-Four Box Set Books 6-10
Forty-Four Box Set Books 11-13
The Road Not Taken: A Prequel

The Rose City Thriller Series (with Emily Jordan)

WHISKEY RAIN: A Rose City Novella
WRONG AS RAIN: A Rose City Thriller (Book 2)

The Broomfield Bay Mystery Series (With Meg Muldoon)

Ginger of the West: A Witches of Broomfield Bay Mystery

ABOUT THE AUTHOR

Jools Sinclair is a bestselling author, teacher, speaker, and creator of *See the Beauty*, a program that helps people celebrate the beauty in their lives. She lives in Tucson, Arizona. Learn more at SeetheBeautyProject.com.